A Basingstoke scene in quieter days. The town's main bus operator was Venture Ltd. which later became a part of the famous Red & White group. Venture once favoured Thornycrofts – indeed there was a financial link between the two – and a pair of A2-Long vehicles of 1927/8 are seen in the garage yard. The chassis were, of course, built in Basingstoke itself but the bodies came from the Acton factory of the celebrated coachbuilding company of Strachan & Brown.

VINTAGE BUS

ALBUM
NUMBER TWO

EDITED by KEN BLACKER

an MHB Book

Frederick Warne

FOREWORD

WHEN the first *VINTAGE BUS ALBUM* (or *ANNUAL* as it then was) went to press we sat back in some trepidation wondering just how well it would be received. Would it prove popular enough and stimulate sufficient sales to justify a *No 2* in due course? There was, after all, no shortage of new bus books from a variety of publishing houses, but ours may possibly not appeal to the important younger element of the market in dealing mostly with happenings from vintage years beyond their recall. We need not have worried, for the support was instantly encouraging and, as proof, here is *Volume 2*.

As was to be expected some articles were better received than others, or at least we assume that they were but we can only judge by the size of the post bag on each. And the response was surprising in that some subjects which we thought were perhaps of less interest proved particularly popular and vice versa. Stan Lockwood's article on the London coach stations of old proved particularly appealing, perhaps because the coaching scene of those days had an aura of glamour which even today is not forgotten, having been passed down through the generations by word of mouth and by authoritative articles such as Stan's. The piece on Belfast's first trolleybuses also stimulated a good response, perhaps because, as one writer to us stated, there has been a dearth of material on Irish matters over the years.

The survey of independents in Bury St Edmunds during the fifties apparently evoked many memories, not to mention a nostalgia for the many interesting types of bus that are not so very long gone from our view. George Robbins' article on General's private hire fleet was popular, as good London articles always are, and another favourite was John Nickel's review of the famous White Rose fleet in Rhyl. Thanks to all readers for their kind and encouraging comments and especially to the press reviewer who thought our collection of bus 'stories' was *marvellous*.

The only sour comment, and this from more than one reader, was on the inclusion of modern day vehicles in the three-page Past Year feature. We make no apology for this. True, ours is primarily an album devoted to bus days gone by, but even Metrobuses and such like will be old one day and it would be wrong for us to completely ignore history in the making. One day even South Yorkshire's DAB and MAN articulated buses will be gone from our midst and they may then be viewed with as much nostalgia as some of us today view the Leyland Titan and Dennis Lancet (the mark 1 versions of each, of course, not the new upstarts with the same names – but isn't it odd how history sometimes repeats itself?). Your editor recalls, not so very many years back, when the MCW organisation brought out its ghastly cheap-looking Orion body, thinking that the bus industry had sunk as low as possible and that no one would ever hold vehicles like these in high regard. Yet Orions are now considered collectors' items which just goes to show, you never can tell what quirks history may take.

The sick and benevolent fund of Crosville Motor Services benefited from our *Volume 1* thanks to the generosity of one of our contributors who donated his fee. Benefit was mostly, however, confined to the pleasure that our readers clearly received from the articles themselves and from the many aspects of fresh information on a variety of subjects that they contained. We sincerely hope that this new volume will be as well received and we look forward, once again, to receiving your comments and suggestions.

Some readers of Volume 1 asked that future issues should contain more articles on preservation. Alas, space limitation is the big problem. Many interesting buses have been saved since the bus preservation movement came into being exactly a quarter of a century ago. This Leyland Lion – representative of a classic model of the mid-twenties – was brought back from Jersey by the Editor in 1958 and is now amongst the varied exhibits at the East Anglia Transport Museum, Carlton Colville, near Lowestoft. It carries the livery of its original owner, Blythe & Berwick of Bradford.

CONTENTS

RED ROSE
Express

**The Road Traffic Act of 1930 was designed to encourage coordination
and eliminate competition, and that is the way things stayed
for nearly half a century. But once upon a time it was a case of free-for-all
on many of the trunk express routes. Rivalry between coach operators
was intense and the travelling public enjoyed an unprecedented choice of facilities,
a standard of comfort and a bargain rate in fares. STAN LOCKWOOD recalls
the companies, many long since vanished, that brought colour and vitality
to two of the main London to Lancashire runs in days gone by.**

'MANCHESTER, sir? Certainly. I can offer a selection of companies, and a choice of four different routes – and you can join the coach in South London, the West End or King's Cross.' No, not the wistful musings of a present day booking agent in the London area, but an actual fact 50 years ago. When the prodigious and exciting build-up of express motor coach routes reached its peak in 1930 the capital was linked to Lancashire by a whole host of operators. Seven concerns served Manchester and district, five ran to Blackpool and seven worked to Merseyside – but space will only allow mention here of those who reached out to London from the cotton capital and the Fylde Coast. The story of the Liverpool contingent must be told another time.

One of the first – if not the very first – to venture on the road south was Manchester-based Eniway Motor Tours of 81A Peter Street, run by two partners, Fred Davies and R Kershaw.

An AEC Regal in Yelloway colours loads for Blackpool with onlookers watching the efforts of the driver throwing a suitcase onto the roof prior to stacking – or is it falling off? Note the two high-positioned sidelamps level with the destination indicator, and the front tyres which would hardly pass today's stringent inspections.

One of Eniway Motor Tours' two Reo Pullman 22-seaters which inaugurated the Manchester-London express run is seen passing through Cheadle. They were later joined by a 20-seater Studebaker. Scheduled journey time for the complete run in 1928 was 9¼ hours.

Lacking the finesse of a present day travel office display, this 1930 window of Holt Bros (Rochdale) Ltd was, nevertheless, very informative. The company's extended tours, removal business, and the Rochdale-Torquay _Devon Express_ are well publicised, in addition to the regular Blackpool-London run.

Initially, two Reo 22-seater Pullman saloons worked a daily service, leaving both cities at 8.30am and travelling via the fairly direct Newcastle-under-Lyme, Birmingham, Coventry and Dunstable route, the Central London Coach Station off the Euston Road being the southern control agents. Ere long, in September 1928, an extra timing was instituted on Monday to Saturday at 10.30am ex Manchester and 10am northbound and, by the following year, an overnight service was in operation. Coaches left both terminals at 11pm and gave connections to and from Glasgow at through fares of 35/- (£1.75) single and 58/- (£2.90) return, passengers changing at Eniway's Peter Street office on to the daily Glasgow run of Lowland Motorways Ltd. This latter Scottish company commenced its Manchester express service on 1st June 1928, running via Carlisle, Kendal and Preston with 20-seater Leyland Lioness coaches to start with, and later with 26-seater Leyland Tigers. Departures were from St Vincent Street, Glasgow, at 9am and Manchester at 8.30am, with an overall timing of 10½ hours, with an additional night working scheduled during the summer months. The availability of a more or less direct connecting service by the two operators proved fairly popular until the advent of the 16 hour direct Glasgow-London run of Midland Bus Services at lower fares.

Eniway Motor Tours became a private limited company in May 1929, but several competitors had appeared on the Manchester-London road by then and Eniway was forced from the scene with the company in liquidation in 1930. Also early in the picture was the old-established business of Holt Bros (Rochdale) Ltd, who coined the famous fleet name Yelloway. Dating back to the earlier removal and haulage operations of Robert Holt, the original company was formed in 1915, and the fleet name of Yelloway itself goes back to the solid tyre days. Holt Bros' service to London started from their garage in Central Drive, Blackpool, at 8am and travelled via Black-

A Yelloway of slightly later vintage than the Regal is this characterful Leyland Cub. The handsome and distinctive fleetname, with its rising sun effect, remained a feature of the company's livery for many years.

burn and Accrington to the company's head office in Weir Street, Rochdale, before picking up at Oldham and Manchester. The coaches then proceeded by 'the prettiest route' – to quote their advertising – by way of Macclesfield, Leek, the Derbyshire Dales, Leicester and Northampton to terminate at the Central London Station. The return journey left at 9.45am and, by 1930, an overnight journey was also in operation. The northern end of the service was then split. The through Blackpool coach took the Manchester, Bolton, Preston and Lytham road while a feeder connected at Manchester to serve a host of East Lancashire towns, taking in

The Christopher Dodson coach body of 1928 for Palanquin was square in appearance but eye-catching in its striking fawn and brown livery. Six of these Leyland Tigers inaugurated the service, one being seen here at London's Bush House. The service was not financially successful and within two years Palanquin was bankrupt.

Majestic chose to travel via Birmingham in linking London with Manchester. Their three Crossley Eagles accommodated only 24 passengers in a high degree of spaciousness and luxury, but their 4 cylinder engines would have rendered them sluggish in comparison with the 6 cylinder machines favoured by their competitors. The full front of the Spicer-built body was an advanced styling feature for the time.

Land Liners' Strachan-bodied Guy FCXs were maximum length 30-footers and were very impressive and heavy looking coaches. The continuous slope of the front end and the full width cab put them years ahead of their time in appearance. There were ten berths in the lower deck and eleven upstairs.

Lower Mosley Street bus station in 1929. This property, acquired in 1928, was the Manchester starting point for North Western's London run. The vehicles in view here are a couple of 1928/9 Tilling-Stevens B10As in use on services of a more local character, together with a Barnsley & District Leyland Lion preparing to head across the Pennines to Doncaster. Nowadays the scene at this point is entirely altered.

Oldham, Shaw, Milnrow, Rochdale, Bacup, Rawtenstall, Haslingden and Accrington to terminate at Blackburn. Such was the amount of traffic, though, that invariably through vehicles served these destinations. The company carried a large number of intermediate passengers and with the London control in the hands of the Central London Station many a muffled curse was uttered by that station's booking staff (myself included) when, at busy periods, we were inundated with postal applications to exchange Yelloway return vouchers for actual tickets for passengers returning north from Northampton, Leicester and Derby. At one time it was Holt's practice not to issue open return tickets, and vouchers had to be sent to London for charting when passengers knew their date of travel. In the early days Tilling-Stevens were the mainstay of the fleet and many a time have I stood at Bignell's Corner (between Barnet

and St Albans), camera in hand, to try and capture a picture of a convoy of Yelloways belting along the London road, resplendent in their fawn and brown livery. In 1928 this operator was running thrice daily between his office at The Mumps, Oldham, and Blackpool, and the following years saw it operating four times a week between Rochdale and Torquay, a journey scheduled at $13\frac{3}{4}$ hours for 27/6 (£1.37½) single and 42/- (£2.10) return. Fares are a trifle higher today. In 1930 Holt's went broke, but fresh capital was injected to keep the business going and the present company, Yelloway Motor Services Ltd, was formed in 1932. Yelloway have given up the London run in recent times but their other express operations still thrive.

One operator which catered specifically for Mancunians was Palanquin Coaches Ltd, a London-based concern which started a service in 1928. To my mind all those years ago the varied fleet names adopted by the pioneers conjured up all sorts of visions, but none more imaginative than Palanquin – 'closed carriage of the East'. Six Leyland Tigers with Christopher Dodson bodies were put on the road, very smart vehicles indeed in a pleasing fawn and black livery with interior fittings which included leather upholstery, curtains and lavatory compartment. The first coach, duly garlanded, had a bottle of champagne broken over its radiator in a christening cere-

mony at Bush House, Aldwych, carried out by a stage personality of the day before the inaugural journey north. Palanquin chose a most interesting route via Bedford, Kettering, Leicester, Derby, Matlock and Buxton, with the Manchester terminus at their agent's office at 14 Piccadilly. London control was in the hands of Road Travel Bookings Ltd of Bush House, Aldwych, one of the big agency networks in the metropolis.

The years 1928/9 saw newcomers entering the express field in increasing numbers, and it was then that Majestic Saloon Coach Tours of 9 Oxford Road, Manchester, joined the happy band on the London run. Soon to become Majestic Express Motors Ltd, the company worked day and night services between the two cities – the day service travelling via Newcastle-under-Lyme, Birmingham, Warwick, Banbury and Oxford, and the overnight run going by way of Birmingham and Towcester. Initially three Crossley Eagles with 24-seater full-fronted Spicer bodies – very advanced styling at the time – and complete with lavatory compartments were included in the company's small fleet, but later on AEC Regals were introduced. The southern terminus was the London Terminal Coach Station in Clapham Road, but in 1934 Majestic Express had joined the London Coastal fold and was working out of the new Victoria Coach Station.

The success of the London-Lancashire coach operations depended largely upon the efficiency of the companies' agents, and Arthur Christy's booking office in Bolton looks all set to do good business. Christy acted as agents for other services besides the London one and they also operated their own fleet of eleven coaches locally until acquired by Ribble in April 1938. The gentleman in front of the Leyland Tigers carries a colourful umbrella as an advertising gimmick for the company's Blackpool express route.

Tognarelli's Pullman Comfort Coaches was another contender on the lucrative Manchester-London road. Bolton-based J R Tognarelli & Co had established haulage services in 1911, but did not enter the passenger field until March 1927 when local bus services radiating from Manchester and Bolton were started. The London service was operating in 1929, departing from Town Hall Square, Bolton, at 8.30am and 45 minutes later from Manchester, returning northbound at 9am. However, this operation was short-lived, the service ceasing when Tognarelli sold out in December of that year. The company started off with a bang and during its first 18 months of passenger activity acquired a fleet of ten ADC 32-seater saloon buses to maintain the half hourly Bolton-Manchester and hourly Manchester-Chadderton services. For tours and private hire some 16 or so 'all-weather' vehicles were on the strength, ranging from two Leyland

Lioness 26-seaters, and Straker-Squire, ADC and Leyland 32-seaters, to a Stewart 14-seater and a couple of similar-sized Buicks. When the firm disposed of its passenger business in 1929 the local bus services were divided between Lancashire United Transport and the Corporations of Salford, Manchester, Bolton and Oldham.

Mention must be made at this point of a particularly unusual and enterprising London-Manchester service that was doomed to failure from the start. It was the brainchild of a Middlesex-based concern, Land Liners Ltd of Edgware, who took delivery in July 1929 of a couple of Guy six-wheeled double-deckers for operation on an overnight service between the two cities. Instead of the conventional seating arrangement, they incorporated 21 sleeping bunks in two and four berth cabins. For a fare of 15/6 ($77\frac{1}{2}$p) single or 30/- (£1.50) return customers were supplied with bed and breakfast as well as their journey, the kitchen compartment for the preparation of breakfasts being located on the lower deck between the two driving axles. The downfall of the service lay in the lowness of the fares combined with the very low carrying capacity of each vehicle. The limited utilisation of expensive sleeper coaches working only nine hours out of 24 for six nights a week was not an economical proposition and Land Liners quickly faded away.

Up to 1929 the independents held sway on the road to London, but then the combine jumped on the bandwagon. On 2nd August of that year two territorial companies, the railway-associated North Western Road Car and Birmingham-based Midland Red started a joint service between Manchester and the metropolis, running by way of Macclesfield, Stafford, Birmingham, Coventry and Oxford. With a daily southbound departure at 8.45am from Lower Mosley Street and a similar return timing from 1A Lupus Street, Pimlico, the overall journey was scheduled to take $10\frac{1}{4}$ hours. Up to then the fares charged by the small companies between the two cities had been 16/6d ($82\frac{1}{2}$p) single and 30/- (£1.50) return, but the combine announced lower fares of 15/- (75p) and 25/- (£1.25) and the others had to fall into line. For many years these standard rates remained unchanged.

Competition was certainly hotting up on this trunk route when Finglands of Manchester made their entrance in late 1929. The road chosen by them gave yet another option to would-be passengers with the vehicles travelling by way of Altrincham, Rugeley and Lichfield to Coventry and Dunstable. Using 26-seater Tilling-Stevens, complete with lavatory and radio, and working out of the Central London Station, Finglands soon became a firm favourite. Lancashire operators who fitted wireless sets in their coaches reported increased bookings and, with its growing popularity, Philco Radio appointed Finglands as Lancashire agents in 1934, a special exhibition coach being made available. The large number of passengers booked on the service was partly linked to the regular visits Charlie Fingland himself made to London to chat with booking staff. I well remember his calls on us at Central London Station and listening with interest to tales of his early beginnings in 1907 when a Rolls-Royce employee. He started a taxi service from Lloyd Street, Rusholme, and after the First World War, in 1921, formed Finglands Garage Ltd with himself and Annie Fingland as directors. A well-patronised hire-car business was operated, together with chauffeured limousines for weddings, funerals, etc. In 1929 Charlie purchased his first coach, a Leyland Tiger, to run excursions and private hire. Soon afterwards he acquired Fleet Motors in St Peter's Square, an operator running a mixed bag of Maudslays, Crossleys and Leylands, and then started his London express service. With the purchase of 76 Great Bridgewater Street as a coach station he formed Finglands Bookings & Coach Station Ltd, but then came the sad day in 1933 when Charlie Fingland died at the comparatively early age of 54. The family business carried on and a London office was opened at 69 Southampton Row and, following the demise of the Central London Station, the southern terminus was moved to the London Terminal Station. In 1936 the premises at Great Bridgewater Street and the London express licences of Fingland's Hire Cars Ltd were sold to North Western but private hire and the excursion business continued from a depot in Wilmslow Road, Rusholme, purchased five years earlier. After the war normal operations resumed and were developed by the acquisition of South Manchester Coachways, the company being re-organised as Finglands South Manchester Coachways Ltd. More recently, in 1971, the entire shareholding of C Holt Ltd was purchased and they, in turn, had taken over the licences of other old Manchester operators such as Sharps, Fred Corkill and Stockport Coachways. Today genial Bob Bunning directs Finglands' operations. His father, who had been the company's general manager for a number of years, bought a

John Bull sold out to Ribble on 15th April 1932 and so did Bracewells. Another of John Bull's activities had been the regular 'Yorkshire Express' Blackpool-Leeds service jointly worked with Walker, Taylor & Sons (Pride of the Road) and W Armitage & Sons (Progress Motor Coaches), both of whom also capitulated on the same day. An AEC Regal of the latter firm is seen carrying the destination 'Huddersfield' but the vehicle is far from its normal route at the *Whoop Hall Inn* near Kirby Lonsdale, possibly on a private hire trip.

WHOOP HALL INN
SOLE PROPRIETOR
TOM. D. NEWELL.
E. NEWELL LICENSED TO SELL.
ALES, WINES, SPIRITS & TOBACCO
TO BE CONSUMED ON OR OFF THE PREMISES
PROGRESS
YORKSHIRE EXPRESS
BLACKPOOL, HUDDERSFIELD, DEWSBURY, BRADFORD & LEEDS
PROGRESS
FRESHMENTS
AS HAM & EGGS.
COMMODATION

One of the extremely rare occasions when Big Ben's Westminster clock tower was seen covered in tons of scaffolding, and the equally rare event of a long-distance coach parked within hailing distance of the Houses of Parliament. What the particular reason was is not known but the Standerwick Leyland Tiger carries a canvas slogan 'The Roads Are Yours, Use Them'. Fitted with a Duple 28-seat body for the Blackpool–London run, the vehicle was new in 1933 and saw fifteen years' service before being sold in 1948.

majority shareholding in 1952, and on the death of Robert Bunning Senior in 1965, he became managing director.

Reverting to the pioneering days, the last independent operator to reach out to London from the Manchester area was Joseph Roscoe & Co, working from Moor Lane, Bolton. Day and night services were instituted, with the overnight run extended to serve Preston. Although a latecomer, Roscoe's soon gained a reputation for being a very fast service, and I bore witness to that fact one summer afternoon in 1931 when the Central London Station was at its quietest. The peace was suddenly shattered by two long blasts from a horn, and to the surprise of the staff present a fully loaded Roscoe's AEC Regal swept into the station – time 4.30pm. Working the 9.15am ex Bolton (10am out of Manchester) and travelling the orthodox Wolverhampton and Birmingham route, the jubilant driver explained that an exceptionally clear road had enabled him to arrive some $2\frac{1}{2}$ hours before schedule – so much for the then ridiculous 30 mph speed limit!

Whilst the Manchester–London services were being opened up, other trail-blazers were at work pioneering routes between the Fylde Coast and the capital. Yelloway has already been mentioned and the four other operators who settled down to maintain regular London schedules out of Blackpool were all north country concerns and, in alphabetical order, they were John Bull, Scout, Smith & Bracewell and Standerwick. There was little to choose between them – they were all so well-publicised, the service offered was impeccable, the vehicles absolutely luxurious, and the amount of traffic they carried knocked most other long-distance routes into a cocked hat. All introduced their London express runs in 1928 but the origins of the Standerwick concern stemmed from pre-First World War days when Ernest Victor Standerwick, a native of Manchester, and his brother Walter operated separate charabanc businesses in Blackpool, beginning with horse-drawn landaus and wagonettes. Taking out his first driving licence in 1909, E V Standerwick made claim to be the first to take a passenger-carrying vehicle from Blackpool to London when, in 1912, he drove a party on an eight-day tour,

taking two days to reach 'the smoke' with an overnight stop at Leicester. In 1925, he and his brother formed W C Standerwick Ltd, but Walter died in 1929 and the business continued under the control of his widow and brother Ernest. The London service initially worked southbound at 8am from King Edward Garage, Chapel Street, on Mondays, Wednesdays and Fridays, returning at 8.30am on Tuesdays, Thursdays and Saturdays, but before long a daily run was in being. The company operated as Standerwick Pullman Lounge and ran via Blackburn, Bolton, Newcastle-under-Lyme, Lichfield and Coventry. The terminal point and London control was in the hands of MacShanes Motors Ltd (the Liverpool–London operator known as MacShanes Parlour Cars) at 53 Woburn Place, Russell Square. In November 1932 the company was acquired

by Ribble but Ernest continued as manager of the subsidiary until 1945 when, following his retirement from active day-to-day management, he was appointed a director. Mr Standerwick saw his company's fleet grow from some eleven vehicles in the 1930s to more than 100 when he died in 1962.

1928 also saw the introduction of Smith & Bracewell on the Lancashire–London run. With offices in Vance Road, Blackpool, and the Crown Garage at Colne, the route originated from both these points, merging at Blackburn to take in Bolton, Knutsford, Cannock, Walsall, Birmingham and Coventry. Invariably, coaches ran through to and from Accrington, Burnley, Nelson and Colne as well as the Lytham and Blackpool service, but on the occasions when only a single vehicle was required passengers changed at Blackburn. Travellers

from front to back which carried roof lights. In all, there were some 20 interior lamps, and with the provision of parcel nets, rug rails and glass-topped folding tables, passengers appeared quite snug when the hood was in position. Only 20 persons were accommodated, the seats being upholstered in best furniture hide and arranged in pairs on one side of the gangway and singly on the other, with longitudinal seats over the wheel arches. Being rightly proud of this vehicle, in a livery of yellow with a red waistband, the operator had the head of a tiger painted on each side, but in subsequent saloon models this was changed to a bulldog with 'John Bull' underneath. The company worked a very popular daily service, with similar timings to Standerwick and Smith & Bracewell until 15th April 1932, when the London route and excursions from Blackpool, based at the head office in the town's Coronation Street, were acquired by Standerwick. On the same day, John Bull's partners in a joint service operated between Blackpool, Huddersfield, Bradford and Leeds – Progress Motor Coaches of W Armitage & Sons Ltd, based in Blackpool's Dickson Road, and Pride of the Road, owned by Walker, Taylor & Sons Ltd of Albert Road – also came under the Ribble banner.

The last of the famous five working out of the nation's pleasure capital to the metropolis was Scout Motor Services Ltd, founded in 1919. In the early years Scout operated private hire and excursions from a depot in Eldon Street, Preston, but in 1928 premises were obtained in Foxhall Rd, Blackpool, just off the Promenade. In November of that year the company inaugurated their daily London express run, followed by an overnight service in 1929. Timings were 8am and 9.30pm southbound, returning at 8.30am and 10.15pm from the Central London Station, with a route through Lancashire via Chorley, Wigan and Warrington – as opposed to John Bull's road through Blackburn and Bolton – and continuing by way of Stafford, Cannock, Walsall, Birmingham and Coventry. Of the five operators, only Yelloway and Scout utilised their vehicles to the full by working night services, and seats were always in demand. Scout had a working arrangement with Imperial of Liverpool whereby, on occasions, a partly filled duplicate from Preston would meet Imperial, ex-

originating at the southern end of the route were at times a little confused with the name of this concern, known as C Smiths Motors (O Bracewell) Ltd. Different timetable publications listed the operating company as either Jos Bracewell Ltd or C Smiths Motors – the coaches just gave C Smith next to the destination indicator – so booking staff in the London area termed this useful little service as Smith & Bracewell. Until taken over by Ribble in 1932 the London terminus was at 91 Southampton Row, but once in the combine fold, services were transferred to the new Victoria Coach Station. Ribble operated licences on their own account only up to November 1932 after which the workings were absorbed by their newly-acquired Standerwick subsidiary.

When Wood Bros (Blackpool) Ltd started their John Bull 'Tiger' service to London they used a Leyland Tiger fitted with an 'all-weather' body by local coachbuilders, H V Burlingham Ltd. Nothing unusual in this, one might say, the 'all-weather' being the stepping stone from charabanc to saloon coach and very much in vogue at the time. Indeed, many operators working express services in the late 1920s were still using this type, but although John Bull's vehicle had the conventional 'all-weather' folding canvas hood, the builders had embodied a fixed coachbuilt back which housed a lavatory and folding wash basin screened by a mahogany partition with doors. It was highly unusual to incorporate these modern facilities in a soft-top vehicle, and I would think that only a very, very few were built to this specification. The front bulkhead and the hood supports were fixed, and an overhead board ran down the centre

Wood Bros [Blackpool] Ltd traded under the name John Bull, which was as patriotic as anyone could hope for. Their London express run started with this Burlingham-bodied Leyland Tiger which was equipped with an all-weather hood so that it could be diverted to purely sightseeing work in the summer months. Its external livery was yellow with red waistband and a picture of a tiger's head was reproduced on the side panels. The interior view shows the sumptuous hide-covered seats which were reckoned to be sufficiently high-backed to allow sleep to be indulged in. Only 20 passengers were carried.

Liverpool 11pm, at Warrington and transfer its London passengers before returning to its home base – or *vice versa* when Scout would carry Imperial's overflow. I once returned in this manner from an illuminations visit, changing at Bridge Street onto Imperial at midnight and into London by 6.15am – not bad going for a nigh-on 190 mile jaunt through the industrial Midlands, plus a refreshment stop. All the time our driver desperately strove [*ahem! ahem!*] to keep his powerful AEC Regal within the ludicrous 30 mph speed limit. Scout was another Leyland Tiger operator and, like John Bull, advertised the London route as 'a luxurious Tiger service'. And very smart the coaches were, too, in fleet colours of cream with brown waistband and roof. Following the acquisition of premises in Starchhouse Square, Preston, in 1930, a frequent double decker stage carriage service was started between that town and Blackpool. From 1939 this local service was operated jointly with Ribble, and the London express jointly with Standerwick. The company lasted many years as an independent operator but in December 1961 the share capital of Scout Motor Services Ltd was purchased by Ribble who operated it as a subsidiary until October 1968 when its services were absorbed by Ribble and Standerwick.

Nowadays the National Bus Company's coaches alone link the metropolis to the industrial heartland of Manchester and the funland of Blackpool on a regular basis. Their uninspired and ghostly coat of all-over white contrasts unhappily with the strong, colourful liveries of days gone by. The glamour has all gone.

With competition at an intense level, an appearance of luxury became all-important on the Fylde Coast run. This later John Bull Tiger is also Burlingham bodied but altogether very much more stylish than its predecessor. The toilet compartment is retained but the soft roof is now a thing of the past.

On 26th October 1968 Scout, for seven years a Ribble subsidiary, at last ceased to trade after 49 years in the business. This impressive Leyland Tiger, bought in 1932 for the London service, is a reminder of happier days. Its attractive body is basically Leyland's standard bus design modified with numerous coach refinements including the toilet compartment, luxury seating and roof luggage rack.

A DENNIS REVIVED

This year's look at a preserved bus from the vintage era takes us back
to the glorious London pirate bus days of the mid-1920s
when open-top double deckers abounded in great profusion. The number
of double deckers of the era now preserved is understandably not great,
and even fewer are the opportunities when the public can avail itself
of a fare-paying ride in one of them on summer service.
One of these few exceptions is the late Prince Marshall's famous Dennis 4 tonner,
XX 9591, which GEORGE PERRY sampled when it operated once again
on the streets of London in 1980–81.

THE best thing that buses can ever do is carry passengers, the glorious purpose for which they exist. While we can admire the array of vehicles on display at the new London Transport Museum in Covent Garden, they might as well be fossils, for such is the tightness of the floor plan that moving just one of them sets up such a domino effect that virtually every other must be displaced. Understandably, it is not to be London Transport policy to let them out for occasional jaunts – the long-past days of Clapham, when a handful such as the K, the NS, the LT and perhaps an STL would take part in the May HCVC Run to Brighton, are blessed memory.

Not that we should grumble – the Museum is superbly sited in the heart of tourist London, and the space has been used effectively, the excellent architecture of the old Flower Market building at last revealed to a public at large, rather than a handful of tradesmen. And the static quality of the exhibits, which can be approached but not boarded, was mitigated in the summer of 1980 by the operation of a vintage bus service from the door of the Museum, through the West End to Oxford Circus, a circuit of John Lewis' and a stately progress back down Regent Street. Prince Marshall's 1930 Tilling ST with the bulbous roof dome

Independent and proud. XX 9591 was the newer of two Dodson-bodied Dennises in W H Cook's Dominion fleet in which it ran almost exclusively along the busy Uxbridge Road westwards out of London as it is seen doing here. Dominion was driven out of business in March 1926 through restrictions imposed by the police under the London Traffic Act and their defunct licences were bought by the LGOC, along with the two Dennises, in May of the same year.

After serving with the LGOC subsidiaries, Redburn and Public, XX 9591 returned to the LGOC fold where it stayed until sold off for scrap in 1932. Thirty-eight years later, in a semi-ruinous state on a Wickford smallholding, it was still sufficiently complete to make restoration a distinct possibility. The upper deck is seen just after removal of a roofing of sheet asbestos which had helped to preserve the vehicle through the weather of four decades. The site was overgrown with brambles and extricating the bus from it was a major task.

and outside staircase has been a familiar sight around town during the summer months for some years, although the route it has followed has changed many times. At last, the Vintage Bus Route, service 100, had a real point to it, and was the best advertisement for the new Museum, which appeared to be attracting a fairsized patronage. And the ST was joined in the route operation by a stablemate five years older, the 1925 Dennis in London General livery with the fleet number D 142. So, an opentopper from the open-top era was carrying fare-paying passengers around London again.

The best way to sample the ride is to be accompanied by a small boy. I tried it in late Spring with my lively three-year-old son on a Sunday afternoon when the sun was trying hard and not too successfully to break through the cloud layer. The round-trip fare of 70p represented excellent value, provided that one could grab a seat upstairs, where a completely new impression of London was there for the viewing. On that particularly eventful Sunday there was the old paddle steamer *Caledonia* ablaze on the Thames, to be glimpsed as we trundled along the Strand past Savoy Street, a vigorous anti-police demo in Trafalgar Square, and a Salvation Army marching band in Oxford Street, all bonuses to the scenery. And if that was not entertainment enough, there was the reaction of pedestrians on the street to be considered, their mouths agape as we sedately passed by. At traffic lights the engine note died away almost into silence, and so vibration-free was the tickover, it was

A series of photographs showing body restoration under way at the LPC works in Hounslow. So good was the main lower deck body structure – despite nearly forty years of neglect – that it was only necessary to replace three pillars and a cross-bearer of the original Dodson ones. The upper deck and staircase were, however, newly built although resembling in every way the original structure. During restoration the body was removed from the chassis to enable the mechanical units to be brought into first class running order by Tim Nicholson.

Restoration work on D142 now nears completion and the body has been reunited with the chassis in the LPC workshops. Extensive restoration work of this sort is very expensive indeed. Even back in 1972, before today's present inflation really took off, the project was only viable through the likelihood of obtaining film and promotional jobs to offset the cost.

just as if the power had been shut off. Then, as the amber and green came up, the cone clutch would engage like the bite of a tiger, and the ancient vehicle would judder into forward motion.

My son was ecstatic. How much more exciting it was to peer over the side, feel the wind on the face, wave to passers-by, and to one's own reflection in plate glass shop windows! A ride in a hermetically-sealed DM is a very boring experience by comparison. By the time the journey was completed, and the old Dennis eased itself back into Tavistock Street, the ST was on the stand, with an almost full load, waiting to go. As soon as the smarter passengers saw the open-top Dennis pull round the corner they scrambled down the stairs and onto the street to be first in line to get a fresh-air seat. It then seemed as though the ST was losing more than half its payload to the Dennis. Such is the attraction of an old style bus ride.

The Dennis, registered XX 9591, was supplied to a pirate undertaking, Dominion, when new in 1925. In the following year its proprietor sold up to the LGOC who, not wanting any Dennis buses in its predominantly AEC fleet, quickly passed it on to Redburn's Motor Services in Enfield. In 1928 it became part of the fleet of the London Public Omnibus Company, which was an amalgam of small concerns, but which was to have a short-lived existence in the face of opposition from the mighty General. Thus, by December 1929 the Dennis was back in the General, along with all the other acquisitions from Public. They carried out a major refurbishment of the vehicle, replacing the solid tyres with pneumatics, covering the seats in moquette, and applying the contemporary 'plums-and-custard' livery used at the beginning of the thirties.

It is to this attractive colour scheme that Prince Marshall has restored the bus, and its elegant 48-seat Christopher Dodson body suits it very well. The engine is mounted in front of the cab in what, for 1925, would have already seemed an antiquated style, but it means that the driver can have company in the cab with him should he wish to be gregarious. It was this feature that enabled policemen to ride next to drivers on the old Bs during the 1926 General Strike, although such a contingency would not have occurred to the designers.

The General only kept the bus until 1932, and as bus design advanced very rapidly in those years, it was disposed of as scrap. A smallholder in Wickford near Southend bought it, probably with the intention of turning it into a shed or summer house. In fact, he did nothing with it, leaving it to the weeds and undergrowth on his land. In the Spring of 1970 some children, playing in the garden of the now derelict house, found what they thought was a tram, and told their parents who lived in the adjacent house. Incredulous that a tram could have survived unnoticed in the tumbledown property, the adults went to investigate. In a bramble thicket they found the remains of the old bus, protected not only by the bushes but by a shed on each side, and inside it was the detritus of the years. The main Southend road was only 50 yards from it, but it had gone undetected.

An HCVC member, Len Cole, heard about the discovery and immediately told Prince Marshall, who raced to the spot. He decided that the vehicle must be saved as it was a unique example of a London independent absorbed by the General. There followed a year of delicate negotiations while the trustees of the property sold the land, and the bus could not be removed until all the legal formalities had been completed. The work of restoration began in November 1971 at LPC Coachworks Ltd, Hounslow, and took three months.

Unlike so many similar resuscitations of derelict vehicles, much of the original was incorporated. The Swan Vestas enamel advertisement on the upper deck is exactly as found, as were other advertisements downstairs, the handrails and the seats and cushions. It was discovered that lightbulbs stamped LGOC could still be switched on after nearly 40 years in the wilderness. The paint scheme was not without controversy, as purists prefer off-white to dark cream, although historically its livery is accurate. The bus carries a stencilled route number for 529, a former Public trunk route from Victoria to Winchmore Hill which survived until the LPTB renumbering scheme. The wooden destination boards for the route were supplanted by the words 'Tour From .... LT Museum Covent Garden via Oxford Circus', during the period of the bus at work on its special duty on 100. It is garaged at Nunhead and operated by Obsolete Fleet.

But what makes these buses really different, either from the range of vehicles inside Covent Garden, or some other preserved buses in private hands, is that they are carrying fare-paying passengers, which is what they were meant to do in the first place.

A recent view of D142, which is now one of the best known of all preserved open toppers. Some purists would like to see it back in its handsome Public blue livery or even in the original Dominion red, complete with solid tyres. But practicalities must prevail, and it is in the familiar General red livery that sponsors want to see the vehicle. And solid tyres would hardly be suitable for round-London operations in this day and age.

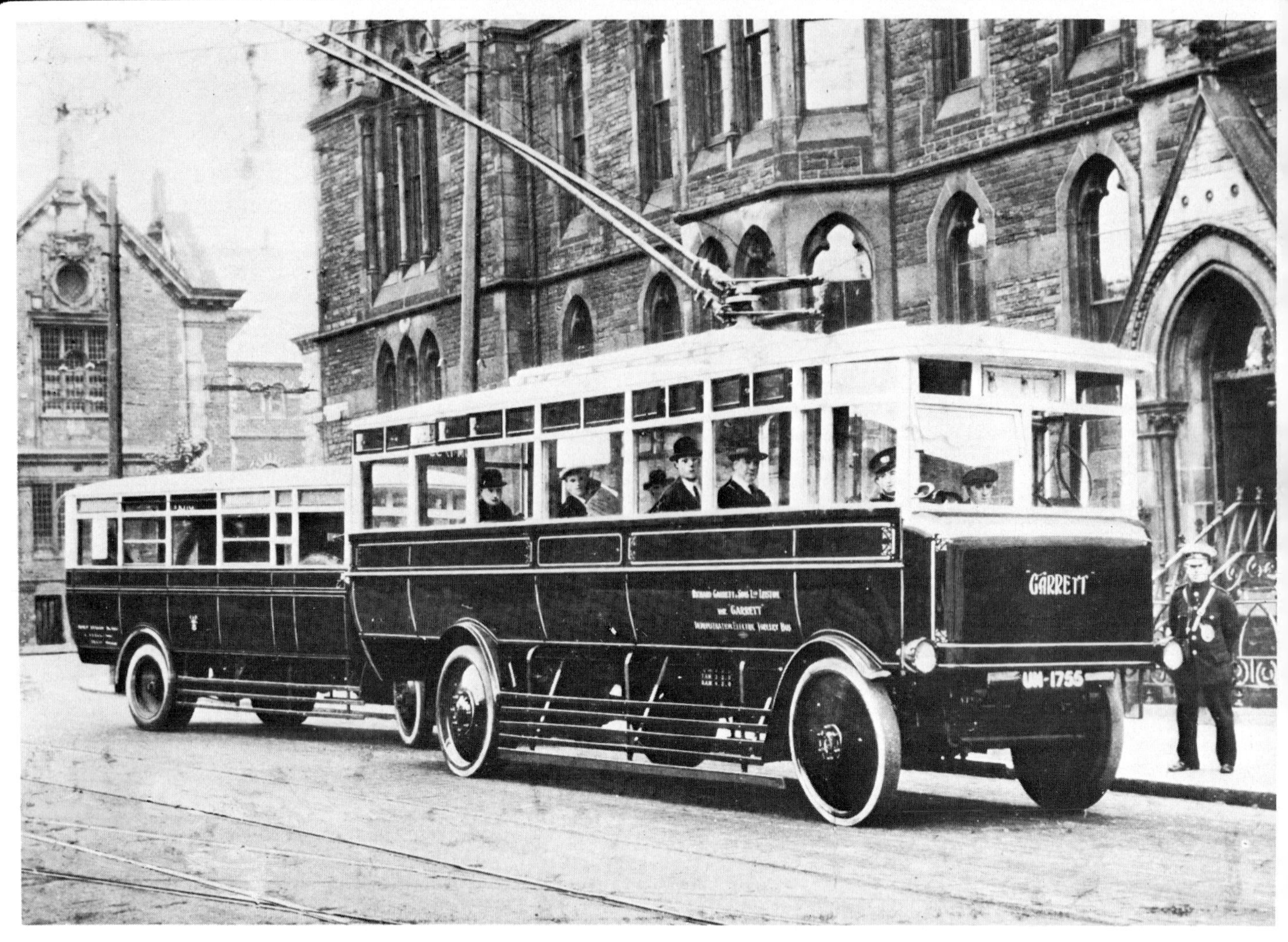

GARRETT TROLLEYBUSES

**Tucked incongruously away in a quiet corner of East Suffolk
was the surprisingly large engineering works of Richard Garrett.
It struggled through good times and bad, and during one of these bad spells
it turned to the manufacture of trolleybuses. KEN BLACKER reveals
how Garrett's trolleybus activities started off with great promise
but faded away almost as quickly as they began.**

SUFFOLK is not a county nowadays associated in any way with the building of vehicles for the motor industry (excepting, of course, the famous Eastern Coach Works bus body plant at Lowestoft) and it seems odd to recall that, back in the nineteen-twenties, it was one of the main trolleybus manufacturing centres in the country. It was a peculiar quirk of history that two completely separate firms engaged on pioneering the spread of the trolleybus were both located in such an unlikely part of the country. They both had much in common, being very old established businesses with their roots deeply entrenched in the design and manufacture of farming implements of various sorts; one was Ipswich-based Ransomes, Sims & Jefferies Ltd and the other, located in the small country town of Leiston some 24 miles from Ipswich, was Richard Garrett & Sons Ltd. This story is about the second of these two.

The origins of the company can be traced right back to 1778 when Richard Garrett set himself up in business at Leiston with a forge at the early

Great hopes were pinned at Leiston on the success of their trolleybus venture and true to expectations the prototype vehicle acquitted itself with credit. Here it is seen during its demonstration tour at the Institute, Keighley, with a Corporation Guy motor bus standing behind.

age of 21. From small beginnings an expanding business grew, thriving through versatility in meeting the needs of farmers in an area of the country where the soil is rich. One generation of Garrett succeeded another and, on 22nd April 1897, a limited company was formed. The nineteenth century saw the production of threshing machines as the mainstay of the company's business although as early as 1856 it exhibited its first steam traction engine at the Chelmsford Royal Agricultural Show. In the first quarter of the present century steam wagons, traction engines and road rollers were high in the company's production list although a prodigious range of other manufactured items kept the Leiston works busy. The nineteen-twenties saw the manufacture of stationary power plant and portable steam engines, threshing machines, electric wagons and dustcarts, diesel tractors, sleeping vans, water turbines, maize shellers, petrol pumps, ice cream freezers and many other items besides.

Soon after the end of the Great War, in 1919, the company became part of the ill-fated Agricultural & General Engineers Ltd group which was formed to combine the manufacturing capabilities of a number of engineering firms in eastern England, including such well-known names as Aveling & Porter, Blackstone, Barford & Perkins, Burrell, Davey Paxman and Peter Brotherhood. Each threw in its lot with AGE on a share exchange basis and, though still controlled and managed locally, ceased to be the ultimate master of its own destiny. These were bad years. The trade depression was severe and the demand for many traditional products, notably steam wagons and traction engines, was declining. AGE and its subsidiaries were struggling and had to find fresh production outlets to survive. Garrett had built an electric van back in 1916, copying such current USA-built models as the Edison and GV, and in 1919 the company went into full production of these vehicles. The profit from building them was not great because a much higher content had to be bought-in than was usual with most Garrett products, but they sold reasonably well and kept some of the work force employed who might otherwise have been put on the dole. It was a natural step from here to

The design of Garrett's trolleybuses was carried out principally by A J Serve, a Frenchman working at Leiston, and his assistant W H Dean. The one and only S type had a very high floor line and steep step, as seen in this close-up of the entrance doorway, but the production O types were lower slung and somewhat improved in this respect.

Newly built but still minus its trolley booms, Strachan & Brown-bodied no 22 is one of a batch of fifteen supplied to Ipswich Corporation in 1926. These differed from all other Garrett trolleybuses in having their front axle set well back in order to make way for an entrance ahead of it.

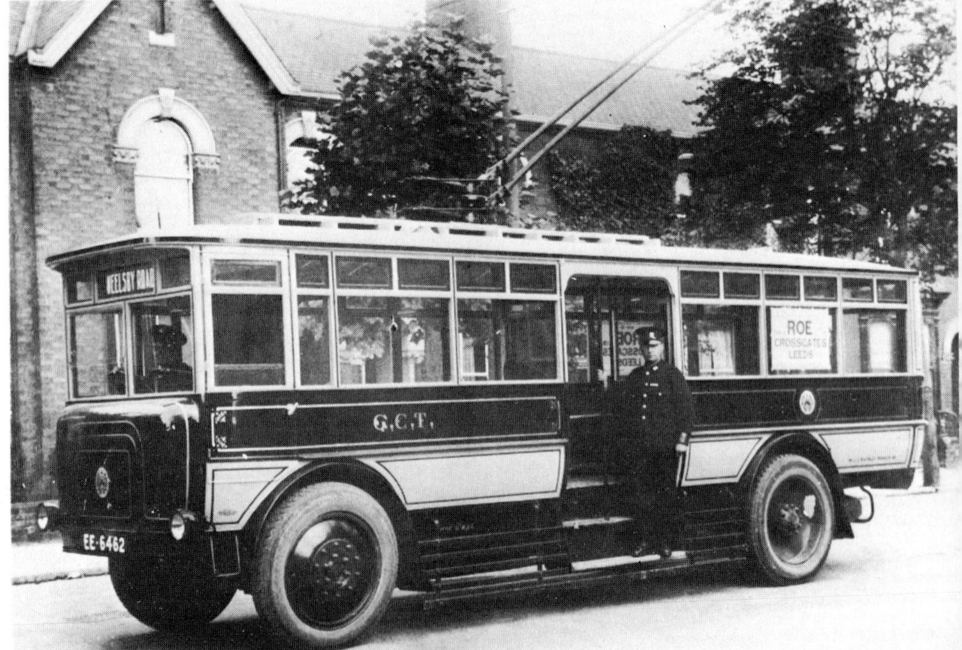

building trolleybuses, a step also taken by Ransomes, Sims & Jefferies, whose Orwell electric vans were arguably more successful than Garrett's. The two firms had long been great rivals, and this rivalry was spurred on by the 1923 trolleybus experiments in Ipswich and the subsequent decision of the town council there to go in for full scale trolleybus operation.

Though the trolleybus had first come to Britain in 1912 its development had been very slow and it was still in a fairly primitive state by 1925 when Garrett built their first chassis. At that time the term 'trolleybus' had not even come into general use, the vehicles normally being referred to as trackless trams, trackless buses, or just plain tracklesses. Because they were regarded more as an appendage to tramway systems than as a serious form of rubber-tyred road transport in their own right, most established vehicle manufacturers paid scant regard to them. By 1925 the only motor builders to include trolleybuses in their production lists were AEC, who dabbled in trolleybuses in a very desultory way, Tilling-Stevens, who gave them up about 1925, and Straker Squire, who were about to go broke! The last-named firm had been the most active of the three because it had forged a close liaison with Clough Smith & Co Ltd, the famous manufacturers and installers of complete trolleybus systems, the vehicles having been supplied under the title of Straker-Clough, and the collapse of Straker Squire in 1926 left Clough Smith searching around for a replacement supplier.

Garrett's prototype trolleybus chassis was built during the summer of 1925 and was duly despatched to the works of Charles H Roe at Leeds for the fitting of a single decker body. Most trolleybuses up to this time had been single deckers of fairly low capacity, and the new Garrett aped the majority of other designs in being a centre entrance vehicle, in this case with the reputedly higher seating capacity of 37. In general, design was well abreast of its time with an underfloor-mounted traction motor and the latest type of foot-operated controller, the latter feature being a big improvement over the tramcar type, hand operated unit usually favoured for early trolleybuses. It very closely resembled AEC's latest trolleybus chassis, also built in 1925, although the AEC was on pneumatic tyres whereas the Garrett was on solids, and both

shared the same type of 50hp Bull traction motor. Bull Motors Ltd of Stowmarket was another AGE subsidiary, so from Garrett's point of view this in-house choice of equipment was a logical one.

The new Garrett trolleybus was designated the S type, though there is no knowing what, if anything, this letter stood for as it appears to have been selected quite arbitrarily. In its red and white livery the new vehicle was demonstrated to a number of trolleybus operators including Leeds – where it received its registration number UM 1755 – Ipswich and Keighley. It was while serving with Keighley Corporation between 4th and 11th July 1925 that it was inspected (on the 10th) by tramway managers from all over the country. After finishing at Keighley, UK 1755 moved to Bradford for an

extended period of demonstration, being subsequently purchased by the Corporation as its no 536.

UM 1755 was clearly successful, being capable of maintaining a steady 25mph in normal service, but the design required certain modifications prior to commencement of a production run. A second prototype was constructed but this one had a substantially redesigned chassis frame. Instead of the completely straight side members of its predecessor, which resulted in an unduly high floor level, the new vehicle was lower built, necessitating the use of a cranked frame over the axles. The frame itself was assembled at Leiston of high tensile pressed steel with silico manganese steel springs and worm driven fully floating rear axle. A 500 volt 50hp Bull motor was again fitted, as was an enclosed type BTH

NESA (*Nordsjaellands Elektricitets og Sporvejs Akieselskab* in Danish) ran its Garrett trolleybuses for an unduly long span of life. No 6 is seen in Copenhagen in its early days towing a neat little trailer; the curtained windows are an unusual refinement for a vehicle on local work. The second shot of a NESA vehicle depicts no 5, curtain and trailerless, which is the vehicle now residing – and occasionally working – at the East Anglia Transport Museum.

Ipswich Corporation specified solid tyres, but these were the last to be fitted by Garrett to new trolleybus chassis. Delivered over a five month period between March and August, the fifteen Garretts became nos 21–35 in the Ipswich fleet. They had 31-seater bodies built at Acton by Strachan & Brown and were notable for having separate front entrance and rear exit to make them suitable for one-man operation.

Meanwhile other orders were coming in. Bradford Corporation, having already gained operating experience with the Garrett demonstrators, decided to order three Roe-bodied vehicles which were delivered as centre-entrance 31-seaters in 1926 (fleet numbers 532–4). The Corporation had also tried out the AEC demonstrator and had found it satisfactory, so a trio of Strachan & Brown-bodied Associated Daimlers were ordered in addition to the Garretts, but all six standardised on Bull motors. Five Roe-bodied O types, almost identical to the Bradford batch, went to Grimsby Corporation as its numbers 1–5 for the opening of its small trolleybus system on 3rd October 1926, and an interesting order for five left-hand drive chassis was received from the North Zeeland Electricity & Tramway Co Ltd (NESA) of Copenhagen, for which Strachan & Brown built the bodies. Twenty-nine trolleybuses were built at Leiston in 1926, and Garrett must have been well pleased with their efforts.

1927 was an even more interesting year. Two old customers returned, Bradford to take three more Roe-bodied vehicles (537–9), this time with front instead of centre entrances, and Grimsby for another two (6 and 7). These were identical to the previous five and were the last trolleybuses purchased by Grimsby until modern, AEC double-deckers came on the scene in 1936. The Copenhagen operator also placed a repeat order, this time for three, but these were supplied only in chassis form, bodies being built locally which were a remarkably close copy of the Strachan & Brown ones on the earlier batch. On service in Denmark these vehicles sometimes towed matching trailers and were very impressive to behold. Nearer home, West Hartlepool Corporation took delivery of twelve Roe-bodied Garretts – fleet numbers 12–21 – for the opening of the Seaton Carew trolleybus route in March 1927. They arrived concurrently with a batch of twelve Vickers-

drum type controller and Estler Bros trolley base. Braking was on all four wheels. The new chassis was called the O type and it was subsequently advertised in two versions, a 35-seater on a 14ft 10ins wheelbase or a smaller 30-seater with a 13ft 6ins wheelbase. The O type became Garrett's standard production trolleybus, though details of the specification differed slightly from order to order according to the purchasers' whims, some being fitted with 60hp motors, others with Garrett's own 10-speed plus reverse controllers, and yet others with trolley bases of the more conventional type rather than the Estler product.

The O type prototype was bodied by Strachan & Brown, then the leading manufacturer of the day, and was a 35-seater centre entrance vehicle in a handsome blue and white livery with gold lining. Garrett registered the vehicle themselves as RT 1345 and it went for spells of demonstration with Leeds Corporation and Mexborough & Swinton before ending up, like the first one, at Bradford where it was later taken into stock numbered 535.

Garrett and Ransomes were competing hard for the plum Ipswich order. Ransomes had got off to a quicker start in that their first prototype had been built a year before Garrett's, but in the end both shared equally in the Ipswich contract. Fifteen were ordered from each stable for 1926 delivery, enabling the Corporation to withdraw the whole of its tram fleet between May and July of that year and making it, temporarily at least, the largest trolleybus operator in the country. Whereas the original RT-registered O type had been on pneumatics,

Three of the four St Helen's Garretts are seen in this view, with the fourth just visible on the left. The location is the Town Hall and the occasion was the inauguration of the town's trolleybus operation in July 1927.

bodied Straker-Cloughs which had been ordered earlier but were late on delivery. The Straker-Cloughs were intended for the through service to Hartlepool and were jointly owned by both councils, whereas the Garretts were the sole property of West Hartlepool. The order for the Garretts had been placed in September 1926 and delivery had commenced with remarkable promptness in January 1927. Garrett also received the contract to erect the new overhead throughout the Seaton Carew route, which, it must be assumed, was sub-contracted to specialists in this field.

Like Grimsby, St Helens Corporation went to Garrett for its first trolleybuses. Four 35-seaters (nos 1–4) inaugurated the pioneer service between Prescott and the mental hospital at Nutgrove via Rainhill on 11th July 1927, taking over from motor buses which had temporarily replaced the trams when these were withdrawn four

years earlier after the tracks were found to be worn out. The service was over two miles away from St Helens town centre and the depot, so the vehicles had to employ skate operation to get to and from the depot morning and night. It is not known for certain who built the bodies for these four vehicles; Ransomes have been suggested as a possibility but this seems unlikely.

However, complete Ransomes-built trolleybuses were purchased in 1928 and Garrett never again secured a St Helens order.

The last batch of Garrett single deckers to be bodied by Roe comprised an export order for six fulfilled in the autumn of 1927. These were the farthest travelled of all Garrett trolleybuses, being shipped to Peru for service in the capital city, Lima. These, like all the foregoing, were O types, but by now Garrett was making big strides in trolleybus design as was evidenced at the 1927 Olympia Show held between 17th and 26th November. The centre of attraction on the Garrett stand was a strikingly impressive six-wheeled double decker which the company knew as its OS type.

All twelve of the Garrett contingent for West Hartlepool are seen in this impressive line-up outside the depot shortly after delivery. White walled tyres were a popular though not entirely practical feature of the day with many operators.

St Helens' Garretts saw little more than a decade in public service; indeed one of the quartet, no 2, was withdrawn in December 1936 when still under ten years old. It was retained and specially decorated for the Coronation with hundreds of coloured light bulbs and toured the system as part of the Council's programme of celebrations for the event. It was also used in a local hospital's campaign in 1938 before going for scrap later in the same year.

The large three-axle passenger vehicle was the talking point of the time. The pioneering efforts of Guy, Karrier and ADC in the manufacture of double deck petrol buses to this configuration is well documented, and there had been rumblings from some quarters about trolleybuses of the same layout. Indeed, Ransomes promised to display a six-wheeler in chassis form at the Show. But in building a complete vehicle Garrett had stolen a march over all of them; the company now led the field. For a brief period the Leiston company was in the forefront of commercial vehicle design. Not only had it been the first to display the potentialities of the high capacity double deck trolleybus, but it was also a leader in the application of the double rear bogie to steam wagon design and was busily involved in experimentation with a diesel-powered, McLaren-Benz engined lorry well before Kerr Stuart's famous pioneering efforts. But it takes capital and dedication to stay in the lead and Garrett, with its diversity of interests and a falling market, had neither.

The OS prototype was an impressive looking machine, embodying a modern covered top but employing the old style open staircase. It was a 55-seater and Garrett claimed to have built the body themselves at Leiston. If so, then credit goes to them in having built what might well have been the first

Garrett seem to have been fond of photographs depicting their products impressively lined up. In this view about a dozen of the 1928/9 batch of vehicles for Mexborough & Swinton are seen, the farthest ones fading away in the distance. The bodies were Leiston-built and the complete vehicles cost £1677 each.

metal-framed closed-top double deck body. A front-mounted 60hp Bull motor arranged with series parallel control powered the vehicle which had Westinghouse air brake equipment. The greatest interest lay, of course, in the Garrett-designed rear bogie on which both axles were driven in tandem by a common propeller shaft, and the rear suspension arrangement which consisted of two inverted semi-elliptic rear springs.

The six-wheeler must have cost a great deal in development and manufacturing costs, but it was not built

with any particular customer in mind and none came forward at the Show. However, the design had already sufficiently impressed Doncaster Corporation for them to order four identical chassis which were constructed at the same time as the Show vehicle. The Corporation intended to open its trolleybus system during 1928 and the four Garretts, delivered between January and March, were available in ample time for the 28th August opening. They were joined for this event by an equal number of similar looking Karrier-Cloughs – Karrier now being Clough Smith's new partner – which were Karrier's first six-wheel trolleybuses. Roe composite bodies were fitted to both types; 60-seaters with enclosed rear ends. The Garretts and Karriers were no doubt carefully monitored by Doncaster as to their respective performances; the fact that the Corporation subsequently ordered no other make than Karrier when purchasing new vehicles for the rest of its lengthy trolleybus-operating career pointedly demonstrates which of the two makes it preferred.

Besides the new Karriers for Doncaster, Guy and Ransomes also produced six-wheeled trolleybuses in 1928. But Garrett was the first to get one into service. Towards the end of 1927 the company somehow heard that Southend-on-Sea Corporation was in difficulties with its small, experimental trolleybus service for which it had three single deckers which were proving inadequate. Besides this the tram service, which the trolleys supplemented, was in danger of collapse because of the state of the track. Garrett offered the loan of the Show double decker which was gladly accepted. It entered service in January 1928, being registered by Southend-on-Sea Corporation as HJ 7363. A few months later the Corporation purchased the vehicle and gave it fleet number 104. Meanwhile it had placed an order with Garrett for a pair of OSs, to which it subsequently added another three to allow for route expansion. These five (105–9) were bodied by Garrett as 60-seaters, this time with composite bodies and enclosed stairs, and their delivery commenced in December 1928 and lasted into the early part of 1929.

Meanwhile the O type single decker was still finding patronage. Mexborough & Swinton had found the demonstrator RT 1345 very satisfactory when it was tried out in December 1925, and in June 1927 an order for six Garretts resulted. The first of the batch (379–84) arrived just before the end of 1927 and the rest were delivered in 1928,

allowing for the withdrawal of older and obsolete Daimler trolleybuses. The operator had great expansion plans in mind and in August 1928 it placed an order for a further nine O types, following it two months later with a request for 12 more. These were to be more powerful machines than the original six, with 60hp motors instead of the usual 50hp, and the first batch was later re-motored to bring them into line. Mexborough & Swinton had now ordered 27 Garretts, making them the company's best customer by far. Garrett was now fully committed to building its own bodywork, and all the Mexborough vehicles were bodied at Leiston, though the design – which was now becoming rather outdated – was clearly influenced by their experience of dealing with Roe and Strachan & Brown.

Despite the healthy orders from Mexborough, no further requests for trolleybuses were received at Leiston in 1928 and the only other vehicle produced during the year was a left-hand-drive Garrett-bodied O type intended for overseas demonstration work. No doubt spurred on by its two Danish orders and the one for Peru, the company clearly saw a good market awaiting its products overseas. However, interest at Leiston suddenly waned, and apart from a sales trip to Holland it is doubtful whether the vehicle did anything but gather dust at Leiston.

Garrett lacked the cash flow needed to make a success of the growing trolleybus market, and whilst others pushed ahead – including arch rivals Ransomes – Leiston quickly lost its pre-eminent position and began falling behind. Early in 1928 the trolleybus had seemed so important to the company; now early in 1929 it could apparently no longer be bothered to push its wares and became very reticent about advertising its trolleybuses at all. It never even troubled to include a trolleybus on its stand at the 1929 Olympia Show, the whole of the company's large exhibition being devoted – unwisely, some considered – to its steam-driven products although, as a token gesture, an O type was exhibited at the Municipal Tramways & Transport Association conference in Great Yarmouth in September. As a result no fresh orders were received in 1929 and the only trolleybuses built during the year were those outstanding from the 1928 Southend and Mexborough orders.

The last batch of trolleybuses produced at Leiston was for delivery to Mexborough & Swinton in 1930. They were severely outdated in appearance by this time, and even the omission of the fan lights did little to modernise them.

In January 1930 Garrett received an order from Mexborough & Swinton for a further three single deckers to take its fleet numbers 61–3. The bodies were again built at Leiston, and delivery took place in May and June of the same year. No 61 made an appearance at the Hastings congress of the Tramways & Light Railways Association, running for three days in June under the Hastings Tramways wires. These three were the end of the line for Garrett. They had found that there was little profit to be had from trolleybus manufacture and were unable to devote the money or the drawing office time to modernise the range. AEC had announced its lowline chassis based on the Regent which it intended to produce in conjunction with English Electric and other manufacturers were

Garrett products figure at the Hastings congress of the Tramways & Light Railways Association in June 1930, the last occasion on which Garrett made any public display of its trolleybus products. Mexborough no 61 finds itself hitched up to a Garrett four wheel undertype 6 ton steam wagon.

The Cornhill, Ipswich, in 1932 showing the Corporation's most recently acquired trolleybus, no 45. This was Garrett's former Continental demonstrator and its life in Ipswich was only a short one of six years. Presumably the non-standard (for Ipswich) layout of its centre entrance body contributed to its early demise.

took over in July 1932. The Beyer Peacock group formed a new undertaking, Richard Garrett Engineering Works Ltd, to run the Leiston works. Sadly, bad times struck again and Garrett finally closed down in 1980.

Trolleybus manufacture at Leiston had totalled 101 over a period of five years. These comprised one S type, 90 O types and 10 OS double deckers. Garrett trolleybuses found their way into eight English fleets and two overseas ones. In some they failed to survive the nineteen-thirties but others lasted longer. Most of the Grimsby contingent lasted for various lengths of time through the war, as did some of the original Ipswich batch, one of which survived until as late as 1949. Great credit goes to the Mexborough fleet, which survived almost completely intact into the post-war era despite growing shortages of spare parts, the last not departing for scrap until 1950. Longest lived of all were the Copenhagen vehicles. Extensively modernised about five years after the German Occupation ceased, they survived until the mid-sixties. One of them, no 5, is now back close to home in preservation at the East Anglia Transport Museum in Carlton Colville, near Lowestoft, where it is the lone survivor of the 101 still in working order.

In conclusion, the author would like to acknowledge having called on Bob Whitehead's *Garretts of Leiston* (published by Percival Marshall & Co Ltd in 1964) for some of the background material to this article. Though it does not deal with the trolleybus in great detail, this excellent volume is a fascinating and valuable record.

GARRETT TROLLEYBUS PRODUCTION—1925–1930

Chassis No.*	Model	Regn. No.	Body	Built	Operator
261	S	UM 1755	Roe	1925	Bradford 536 (ex demonstrator)
262	O	RT 1345	Strachan	1926	Bradford 535 (ex demonstrator)
273–287	O	DX 5623–37	Strachan	1926	Ipswich 21–35**
297–299	O	KU 9101/3/2	Roe	1926	Bradford 532–4
300–304	O	EE 6461–5	Roe	1926	Grimsby 1–5
306–310	O		Strachan	1926	NESA, Co'hagen 1–5
312–323	O	EF 3370–81	Roe	1927	West Hartlepool 20–31
325–327	O	KW 204–6	Roe	1927	Bradford 537–9
328–331	O	DJ 5243–6	?	1927	St Helens 1–4
332/333	O	EE 7097–8	Roe	1927	Grimsby 6/7
335–7	O		—	1927	NESA, C'hagen 6–8
338–343	O		Roe	1927	Lima Tramways
379–384	O	WW 4688–93	Garrett	1927	Mexborough 34–39
385/6/8/9	OS	DT 821–4	Roe	1928	Doncaster 1–4
387	OS	HJ 7363	Garrett	1927	Southend 104
392	O	DX 9610	Garrett	1928	Ipswich 45 (ex demonstrator)
393–413	O	WW 7872–80/ WW 8790–8801	Garrett	1928/9	Mexborough 40–60
414–418	OS	HJ 8925–9	Garrett	1928/9	Southend 105–9
425–427	O	WX 4440–2	Garrett	1930	Mexborough 61–3

* The chassis number series commenced in 1919 at 102 and included battery electric vehicles as well as trolleybuses, and these occupied the gaps in the above list. Operators' registration and fleet numbers are not always in the same sequence as the chassis numbers. **Not numbered in order.

poised to follow suit. Garrett could no longer compete; indeed, even its battery electric vehicle production was largely also at an end with the exception of some very advanced, low level refuse collecting vehicles for Glasgow Corporation, which continued to be built at Leiston on and off throughout the thirties. The company was left with one trolleybus on its hands, the so-called Continental demonstrator of 1928. This was converted to right-hand drive and the body was rebuilt as a 31-seater centre-entrance vehicle for home operation. In this form it was sold to Ipswich Corporation in whose fleet it became no 45 in November 1931.

Garrett fared very badly in the financial slump that heralded the new decade. In February 1932 an Official Receiver was put into Richard Garrett & Sons Ltd and a liquidator was appointed in April. Things looked bleak for the Leiston works for a while until Beyer, Peacock & Co Ltd of Gorton

THE PAST YEAR

Once again, in this regular feature, we take a glimpse at recent happenings on the bus scene. We look at the new as well as the old, for what is new today in this ever-changing world of ours will be old tomorrow; history is in the making all the time. Recession has hit the industrialised nations and change is inevitable.

Like all the industrialised nations of the west, Britain is in the icy grip of hard times and the bus manufacturing industry is suffering along with the rest. That there should be some fatalities is inevitable, but it was nevertheless sad to see the famous Park Royal works close in 1980 so soon on the heels of the demise of AEC. Most manufacturers are, however, fighting back and the bus buyer of today can choose from the widest range, both home made and foreign, that has been available for a long time. Even Shelvoke & Drewry is back in the bus world after an absence of many years. The greatest success story of late is that of Dennis, the only British manufacturer in 1981 not on short time working. Their comprehensive range of Dominator, Jubilant, Lancet, Falcon and Dart is selling well. Typical is this East Lancs-bodied Dominator, a 1981 delivery to the A1 consortium based on Kilmarnock. The untidy cut-away rear end styling of this particular vehicle is a feature not found so often on new buses these days.

The greatest impetus for innovation the industry has received for a long time came with the ending of road service licensing for express services on 6th October 1980. Coach operators were quick to exploit their new found freedom, and the British Coachways empire was founded almost overnight [though it has not been without its troubles, a number of participants having later bowed out]. The National network, seemingly in a state of genteel decline, realised that the days of resting on its laurels were over and quickly sprang into action with its own counter-offensive. Many new services and new links have since been created and well-known names now regularly turn up in previously unfamiliar places. Here a Duple-bodied Volvo of Green Line arrives in Cambridge, a destination well beyond the old limits of this operator's services. Also present in the Drummond Street bus station are an AEC Reliance of Premier Travel and an Eastern Counties Bristol RE. The Reliance is one of many whose presence adds a luxurious dimension to stage carriage travel and which have been purchased through the bus grant system now being phased out, whilst the Bristol is an early one of its type and due soon, no doubt, for retirement.

Many of the larger operators, both NBC and municipal, have celebrated Jubilees in recent times, both diamond and golden and – in the case of Royal Blue – a complete centenary of service. These occasions have usually been seized upon as an excuse for reviving old glories by repainting vehicles of today in liveries of yore. The companies within the NBC have been particularly prone to these outbursts of nostalgia, and it has been a sight for sore eyes to witness the revival on the odd vehicle or two of some fine, traditional colour schemes many of which disappeared on an edict from NBC headquarters not so very long ago. A vibrant, enterprising bus company, responsive to and instantly recognisable by its 'own' travelling public, is no place for the stifling, levelling-down effect that the impersonal corporate image can bring. We have recently seen beautifully repainted reminders of the old liveries of Mansfield District, East Midland, Eastern National, Chatham & District, Aldershot & District, Southdown and others. Here an elderly Maidstone & District Leyland Atlantean, back in traditional colours, pays a visit to London Transport's Chiswick Works.

Such is the nature of the industry that there is always a certain amount of coming and going amongst the smaller bus and coach operators, but with the bigger ones the position can usually be expected to remain far more static. Even so some fairly big names have vanished from the scene in the last decade such as North Western, Midland General and MacBraynes, not to mention the many municipal operators lost to us through local government reorganisation and the formation of the PTE's. The latest 'big name' to go, effective from 1st April 1981, was that of Lancashire United, now swallowed up into Greater Manchester Transport. This characterful firm, which retained some of its famous Guy double deckers right up to the end, once even ran a sprawling trolleybus system under the South Lancashire title. This late nineteen-fifties photo at the company's Atherton headquarters includes a then new Orion-bodied Daimler and a typical Northern Counties-bodied Guy Arab. Foremost, however, is a handsome Foden, a particularly appropriate subject in view of the financial collapse of this famous Cheshire manufacturer in 1980 and its subsequent partial revival under American ownership which throws a heavy question mark over its psv production plans.

SEEN & HEARD

SOME INTERESTING RECENT FINDS

A reader has sent us this picture of a 1929 ex-Manchester Corporation no 33, Leyland Tiger TS2. It was sold by the Corporation in 1962 and is still languishing in North Wales . . . . .
At least five ex-London Cubs rotting in a Billingshurst scrapyard have at last been rescued. Two were dug out early in July 1981 and are on their way to new owners whilst the rest will follow later this summer . . . . .
During the autumn of 1980 rescue was made of an ex-Amersham & District Gilford (LPTB GF161) 1660T with Wycombe body. The vehicle lay in an orchard in Old Wives Lees, near Canterbury, since before the war. The London Transport name could still be seen on the side . . . . .
Very early chassis are now hard to find but Barry Weatherhead of Woburn Sands apparently knows of a 1905 or thereabouts De Dion bus chassis still resting underneath a bungalow . . . and last year we went to see a c1911 Straker Squire bus chassis on a farm in metropolitan Essex. The chassis was in good condition . . . . .

Two vehicles that showed themselves briefly at the start of the 1981 Brighton Run but failed to complete it for mechanical reasons were a 1927 Associated Daimler (BR 6496) and 1927 Leyland Lioness (KW 6025). Both had been restored jointly by S H Wyatt, Coachbuilders, and LPC Coachworks to the order of Mr Jim Leake of Muskogee, Oklahoma. The ADC is built as a replica of an all-weather coach with canvas top whilst the Lioness is made to the style of a drop frame charabanc. Both were constructed from original drawings.

Some readers will associate Mr Jim Leake as owner of the previously restored Milnes Daimler ex-Brighton Hove & Preston. This reminds us that Obsolete Fleet are well advanced with the restoration of their Milnes Daimler, a 1906 model ex-London Motor Omnibus Company with body by United Electric Car Co of Preston. Obsolete Fleet say they hope to have it ready for Brighton 1983 . . . . .

At Whipsnade, Michael Sutcliffe is working wonders with the restoration of his 1921 ex-Todmorden Leyland. Most of the chassis is restored whilst the saloon part of the body is rebuilt and in undercoat. When we saw it in the early summer Michael was making the top deck seats and about to fit the staircase.

This London LT (1076) is still being used as a weekend caravan. However, its owner is displeased with enthusiasts who, in recent months, have sawn off the chassis dumbiron plates and taken the bonnet number from the side . . . . .

A derelict Tilling-Stevens B10 which lay for many years at Lyneham, Oxfordshire, was bought last year by Southdown enthusiast Michael Plunkett. Michael intends to incorporate many of the units into his 1928 Southdown B10 (UF 6806) which he hopes soon to renovate . . . . .

A nineteen-twenties Leyland Edinburgh style single deck body has been discovered in the Cumbria region and can be purchased for renovation . . . . .

This old tanker lorry now owned by Andrew Pring was once Timpson no 317 (GN 7317), a 1931 AEC Mercury originally fitted with Harrington C22R body . . . . .

In the Isle of Wight a clear-out of a scrapyard last summer unearthed the remains of a Dennis Arrow coach . . . . .

Huddersfield enthusiast Geoff Lumb is currently working on a 1924 Karrier ex-Premier Transport of Keighley. It will carry a 24–26 seat body by Strachan & Brown. Geoff is in need of a Karrier FC4 engine and any Strachan & Brown body spares . . . . .

O'er Highland Highways

**One of Britain's loveliest yet most remote areas is Scotland's western seaboard
and the great spread of the Highlands lying inland from it. For many years
communications within the area were difficult and costly due to primitive
road conditions, but despite all the hazards a coordinated transport system was built up
by David MacBrayne Ltd, embracing the carriage of passengers and goods by road and sea.
ALAN NIGHTINGALE looks at a decade of development of the company's
road passenger services between 1928 and the outbreak of war in 1939.**

SINCE 1879 the name of MacBraynes has been synonymous with shipping in the West Highlands of Scotland. In that year Mr David MacBrayne took over control of the West Highland Steamers, gaining the Post Office mail contract the year after, and the company continued as a private family business until 1st January 1906 when a lim-

ited company, David MacBrayne Limited, was incorporated in Edinburgh. In 1906 the company started to develop road motor services to complement and feed its steamer routes, starting with a service from Fort William to North Ballachulish and followed, in the period 1911–13, by Inverness to Fort William and Glenurquart,

1931 saw the arrival of MacBraynes' first Bedfords, a make which was to prove so successful for four decades on the company's quieter runs. One of these was required to cater for the local passenger and mail traffic on the Loch Fyneside run, and is seen here bearing the appropriate route board on its luggage rack, 'Inveraray and Tarbert via Ardrishaig'.

The first of the many new Maudslays to join the fleet over the years were a pair of full-fronted Vickers-bodied ML3s delivered early in 1929 for the Inverness-Fort Augustus steamer replacement service. They were soon decreed to be too heavy for the primitive road surface alongside Loch Ness and one of them, ST 5452, was sold before the year was out.

Oban to Ardrishaig and Inveraray to Ardrishaig. Early vehicles included a German Daimler, Albions and Commers and were mainly of 14 seats or less, most roads being unsuitable for anything much bigger, even if the services had warranted it. Thereafter, things remained fairly constant for several years. Although, in June 1925, consideration was given to replacing the Loch Ness mail steamer with road services, several years were to pass before this took place.

The mail contract fell due for renewal during 1928. Operation of most shipping services was completely uneconomic due to the sparse and scattered nature of the population they were serving and the time was fast approaching when the company could no longer cross-subsidise loss-making services because there were so many of them. On 9th February 1928 the Post Office was advised that MacBraynes were considering giving up the contract and most of their services as they had been subject to 'too much unfair criticism' in the past. This prompted the Government into giving financial help, but there was extensive parliamentary objection to the proposed new contract, and on 23rd May MacBraynes wrote to the GPO notifying their withdrawal from negotiations but expressing their willingness to continue until 31st October while other arrangements were made. Within a week the GPO was advised by the Minister of Transport that the LMS Railway and Coast Lines Limited were already trying to mount a joint rescue operation, the main feature being a guaranteed 5% return on the capital cost of taking over. A proportion of this subsidy was to come from the mail contract. A new company was incorporated on 21st October – David MacBrayne (1928) Limited – and on 1st November it acquired the assets of the old company for £77,000. Road passenger services in operation at

Prior to the company's restructuring of 1928, with its accompanying inpouring of fresh capital, MacBraynes' road passenger operations had only been carried out on a minor scale. Two of the vehicles which passed to the 1928 company were these Ford Model Ts, SB 1450 and ST 1888. Their primitive open-sided bodies carry roll-down canvas side screens as protection against the all too often inclement Highland weather.

this time were Oban–Ardrishaig, Ardrishaig–Tarbert, Inveraray–Ardrishaig, Glenurquhart-Inverness and Fort William-North Ballachulish. The last mentioned service had two return journeys a day, the others only one, the timetable carrying the warning 'accommodation limited, seats cannot be guaranteed'. Thirteen passenger vehicles were acquired, believed to have consisted of one Standard, two Commers, four Fords and six Morris-Commercials. Three of the Fords were ST 1854/88 and SB 1450 and the Morris-Commercials SB 2157, 2665/6/98, ST 3035, 4910.

Management consisted of two Boards, a Main Board with representatives of the two owners meeting in London and responsible for policy, plus a Glasgow Local Board which looked after the day-to-day running and organisation of the company's services.

The following year, 1929, was to witness the start of a rapid expansion of road services. In February, withdrawal of the famous Loch Ness mail steamer was sanctioned, Ministry of Transport approval for replacement bus services between Inverness and Fort Augustus and Inverness and Foyers for conveyance of passengers, parcels and mails having been granted the previous December. On Saturday, 6th April, the regular steamer sailed for the last time, the buses taking over from the following Monday. The first new vehicles following the reorganisation arrived for the Fort Augustus service in February and were two forward control Maudslay ML3s (ST 5452/3) carrying 30-seat front entrance bodies built by Vickers; these vehicles were the first of many MacBraynes buses to be fitted with a special compartment at the back for the carriage of mails as well as the first of many vehicles from the Maudslay factory. The livery of red lower panels, ornately lined, cream windows and roof and black mudguards was enhanced by the full company title appearing on the sides with the addition of the fleet numbers and 'Royal Route' insignia perpetuating a famous title from steamer days.

In January 1929 the decision was taken to purchase four new vehicles for the Ardrishaig-Oban service as the start of the summer season was to see the expansion of this old established bus service through the beautiful Pass of Melfort. As part of the rationalisation of steamer services the approval was given in March for withdrawal of the steamers covering the sections of the famous 'Royal Route' between these points, ie, Ardrishaig to Crinan via the Crinan Canal and the Crinan to Oban service. The through passenger service was replaced by an additional return journey on the bus service, this being marked in the timetable as 'Tourist Express Service – through booked steamer passengers only', a feature which survived for the next ten years. By June the four vehicles had arrived, these being forward control Maudslay ML6As, SB 3360-3, fitted with Hall Lewis dual entrance 31 seat bodies and featuring half canopy front domes.

In March consideration was given to future expansion of road services, including provision of Sunday services, and in April the important decision was taken to introduce a service daily between Glasgow and Ardrishaig in direct competition with the Link Lines service between these points started in April 1927 with three vehicles, but by now employing up to eight Reos and Leyland Tigers. New vehicles would be required and Scottish firms were to be given every opportunity to tender; in May it was decided to purchase three six cylinder Maudslays suitable for 20/22 seat bodies at a cost of £1700. Tenders of £1182 for the building of Oban garage and £1440 for one at Ardrishaig were accepted at this time. Also in May the possibility was discussed of opening a service on the island of Harris between Rodel and Leverburgh, only to be rejected two months later as not likely to be profitable. Meanwhile, two of the Fords inherited from the old company (ST 1888, 1854) were sold in June and September respectively.

By August 1929 the vehicles for the Glasgow-Ardrishaig service had arrived, this time normal control Maudslays, SB 3367-9, again with Hall Lewis bodies but with front entrances only and seating 26 passengers. On 21st August MacBraynes joined Link Lines on this service and competition was soon intense, with much support being expressed for the pioneer operator in the letter columns of the local press,

Rakish-looking normal control Maudslays with Hall Lewis bodies were purchased to compete with – and finally annihilate - the existing Link Lines service on the long and tortuous but potentially very profitable Glasgow-Ardrishaig run. All three are seen in the line-up photographed just after delivery, whilst the back end of SB 3369, showing the ladder to the roof rack, is seen on a dreamy day at Inveraray as the vehicle heads, well laden, for Glasgow.

urging intending passengers to 'use Link Lines, the original operator to open up the area with a regular road service link from the Argyllshire villages and towns to Glasgow'. During the summer an offer was received from an Isle of Skye operator, Ronald MacLean of Dunvegan, who wrote stating his willingness to dispose of his hiring business. Consideration was given to the purchase of his Dunvegan and Kyleakin service, but it was decided that it would not be beneficial to the company and so no offer was made.

A serious blow was dealt to the new Fort Augustus mail service in the autumn when Inverness County Council announced restrictions under the provisions of the Roads Act 1920 prohibiting the use of

Most of the MacBraynes operating territory lay in the most beautiful of scenery, and the grimy tenements and office blocks of Glasgow were in distinct contrast to this. In more typical surroundings the third of the batch, SB 4020, is seen heading alongside Loch Fyne on its way from Glasgow to Ardrishaig.

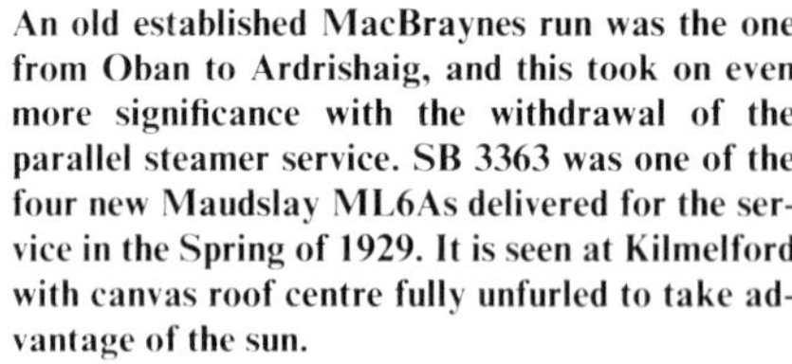

An old established MacBraynes run was the one from Oban to Ardrishaig, and this took on even more significance with the withdrawal of the parallel steamer service. SB 3363 was one of the four new Maudslay ML6As delivered for the service in the Spring of 1929. It is seen at Kilmelford with canvas roof centre fully unfurled to take advantage of the sun.

The four new Maudslay Meteors purchased in 1932 to cover the ex-Link Lines operations were worked very hard on the Glasgow–Ardrishaig run on which they gave very good service. The complete batch is seen at the company's Glasgow headquarters at a special reception ceremony when newly arrived from Park Royal.

heavy vehicles and buses over 14 seats on the Inverness to Fort Augustus road until the road was rebuilt. Orders were hastily placed for four normal control Morris-Commercial chassis to which neat front entrance Alexander 14-seat bodies were fitted. SB 3484-7 cost a total of £2521.10.0d and at least two, if not all four, arrived just in time to beat the 1st December deadline for imposition of the restrictions. As with other vehicles delivered in 1929, roof mounted luggage compartments reached from steps at the rear of the vehicles were notable features. Four vehicles were displaced; a 20-seat Morris on loan from that company was returned, another 14-seat Morris was relegated as a spare and a further obsolete Morris, possibly ST 3035, was to be sold or used for spares. Rather surprisingly, the fourth vehicle declared redundant was Maudslay ST 5452 which, though still less than a year old, was sold to another Coast Lines subsidiary, B & I Lines, for use in Dublin. Its sister vehicle was retained and deployed elsewhere.

After the rather hectic activities of the previous year, 1930 was much quieter. In May it was decided to provide the Foyers service on Sundays. The postal authorities requested an improved mail service to and from Glenurquart and some thought was given to basing the service at the Inverness end which would have required an additional Inverness to Drumnadrochit service during the currency of the winter timetable. However, considerable passenger traffic would have been affected as the service was a busy one and it was estimated that £400 per annum would need to be paid by the Post Office to compensate for loss of traffic. Eventually it was decided to retain the Glenurquart based service but to extend the 11.00am run from Inverness beyond Drumnadrochit to Glenurquart and an additional payment of £100 per annum was made by the Post Office.

On the vehicle scene the only notable event was disposal of accident damaged Ford SB 1450 in January. The passing of the Road Traffic Act in 1930 requiring licensing of all existing and new stage services and advertised excursions and tours was to have a profound effect on future developments.

The following year saw the ordering in April of two new 20-seat buses at a cost of £525 each for the Inverness-Foyers and Inveraray-Ardrishaig-Tarbert services. Although ordered as Chevrolets, the General Motors British subsidiary Vauxhall had just introduced the Bedford range of commercial vehicles and these two buses arrived in the summer in the form of the new WLB model. SB 3832/3 carried attractive Bracebridge front entrance bodies and their arrival was to prove the start of a 40-year association with Bedford chassis. Morris-Commercial SB 2157 was sold in March.

At the request of the Ministry of Transport, the Inverness-Fort Augustus service was altered from 1st April 1931 to leave Fort Augustus in the morning and Inverness in the afternoon. The Post Office asked that the 3.30pm Inverness-Drumnadrochit service be extended to Fort Augustus and this was agreed, the licence being granted from 1st August. With vehicles now remaining overnight at Fort Augustus, ac-

commodation was required and in October land was feued from the local laird for the erection of a garage at a rental of £2 per annum. About the same time it was considered appropriate to build a small garage at Foyers and arrangements were made to secure a piece of land inside the private grounds of the large British Aluminium Company smelting works at a fee of £5 per annum.

In midsummer a private operator in Argyllshire, A W Paterson of Barfad, Ardfern, applied to the Traffic Commissioners to continue his services between Ardfern and Ardrishaig and Ardfern and Oban. MacBraynes objected on the grounds that the services were in direct opposition to their mail service along the route and that Paterson ran his bus just in front of theirs. It is known that by October the licence for Paterson's Oban service was granted but with the stipulation that it should operate at least 30 minutes behind the mail service. Early in 1932 a licence was also granted for the Ardrishaig service.

More significant was objection to the licence for the Glasgow-Ardrishaig service of Link Lines on the grounds that a coordinated timetable should be negotiated between the two parties as 'Link Lines invariably operate their runs a little ahead of MacBraynes' times'. In some quarters it was probably felt that this was justified – after all, Link Lines had pioneered the route! Opposition to MacBraynes was particularly fierce in the Lochgilphead area where it was feared a monopoly would result in a steep rise in fares. By October a meeting had been arranged between the two parties, the Traffic Commissioner being desirous of a coordination agreement. At this meeting it was disclosed that Link Lines were prepared to sell their services. MacBraynes estimated the value of the business to be between £8000 and £10,000 with a rough estimate of the value of the vehicles and plant, which included passenger and goods vehicles, of £6500. The Link Lines shareholders, Messrs W P Naismith and A M Melville, respectively Chairman and Managing Director of the India Tyre Company, Inchinnan, felt that this was not enough. They would not, however, provide any accounts for the business, a factor which had caused earlier negotiations for a takeover elsewhere to be frustrated when Mr Carmichael, an Edinburgh contractor, had attempted to acquire it. Arrangements had fallen through, but not before his cousin, an operator in Dumbarton, had earlier spent a week at Arrochar taking a census of traffic on the service. Carmichael then approached the Paisley based operator Young & Sons in an endeavour to purchase Link Lines through them; these negotiations went the way of the earlier ones.

Discussions on timetables dragged on into 1932, neither company seeing its way to altering theirs in a way satisfactory to the other, negotiations again breaking down. Then, on Wednesday, 17th February, Mr Naismith visited Bailie Thomson of the powerful Scottish Motor Transport Company in Edinburgh, and advised him that Mr Carmichael had made an offer 'in the region of £12,000' and that anyone else had until Friday to make a counter offer. This information was immediately passed to

MacBraynes' manager and hasty communication with the Board members followed, resulting in agreement to ask SMT to make a firm offer 'not exceeding £12,000' to Link Lines on MacBraynes' behalf. Agreement was duly reached whereby MacBraynes would acquire both the passenger and goods services of Link Lines, thereby consolidating their position in Argyllshire. The price paid in the end was £10,000, the bus service proportion being valued by an independent arbitrator at £6880 with MacBraynes taking over responsibility for operations on 1st March. Application was made for continuation of the service with a coordinated timetable; the hearing on 20th April approved the plans and revised timetables operated from 1st May.

Upon takeover, the Link Lines fleet contained seven buses and a charabanc. Five of the buses were Leyland Tiger 26-seaters purchased in 1929 (GE 4585/6, 5242, 5489, 5608) and two were Crossley Alpha 26-seaters (GG 1619/20) of 1931. The charabanc was GE 6601, a Ford. The report of MacBraynes' Chief Engineer on 25th April makes interesting reading. It would seem that, under the pressure of competition from MacBraynes, the Link Lines fleet had been run into the ground, though no doubt the poor road conditions in Argyllshire and the difficult terrain were also factors contributing to their poor condition. One of the Leylands, GE 4586, had received a chassis and engine overhaul and a new body by Midland (Airdrie) at a cost of around £600 in 1932, but the others were found to require complete stripping and repair, little or no attention having been paid to greasing and oiling. New clutches were required and new tyres, the estimated cost being in the region of £690 per bus. It was decided not to take these four Leylands into stock, and the Ford charabanc was also disposed of immediately even though it received the token fleet number 45. Negotiations had apparently been taking place with the Maudslay Motor Company as four new Maudslay Meteors were on offer at £1047 per complete vehicle if the Leylands were given in part exchange. The offer was accepted when it was realized that the cost of repairs would be saved in only two years whilst maintenance costs would be reduced as other Maudslays were already operated. It was decided to retain the rebodied Leyland as a spare bus and also the two Crossleys. Mileage run on the Crossleys was low. Though only a year old, the vehicles had been returned to the makers on several occasions – one had even received a new engine. They were considered suitable for light duty but it was necessary to strengthen the Crossley-built bodies to meet MoT requirements which cost, with a repaint, £125 per vehicle. The report concluded, 'The condition of the fleet, considering its age, is appalling – only because the MoT have been informed that it was the intention to carry out repairs have the buses been permitted to remain on the road'.

The four new Maudslays, SB 4018-21, arrived in midsummer 1932 with full canopy Park Royal front entrance bodies. Bus type seats for 30 passengers were fitted, but these had thick cushions and backs. Other features were luggage racks, heaters (fitted to all subsequent long distance vehicles)

and five half-drop windows each side. The exterior window louvres had names of the main points served on the Glasgow–Tarbert service painted onto them. The entrance door folded inwards, and the roof mounted luggage rack was reached via a ladder at the rear of each bus. These were the first vehicles to carry an additional display glass (above the destination screen) with the wording 'Royal Mail Services' which became a famous MacBraynes trademark. Two more Bedford WLBs were ordered in April for the services from Inverness to Fort Augustus and Foyers at a cost of £1076 to replace obsolete vehicles. ST 6957/8 were delivered by June and had 14-seat Park Royal front entrance bodies incorporating a mail compartment.

Reverting to January, the LMS had requested operation of the additional seasonal service on the Oban–Ardrishaig route as a normal service throughout the year. The General Manager thought traffic to be uncertain, but nevertheless it was agreed to carry out a three-month test, a licence being granted enabling the service to commence on 1st April. Early results were not encouraging, and although the summer traffic was naturally satisfactory, by October the service was running at a loss again and plans were made to discontinue operations for the winter, re-introduction being planned for June 1933. The Traffic Commissioner had other ideas,

however, and so the service continued throughout the winter to further test the situation. In April 1933 the local Board recommended that it should be possible to operate the additional winter service on the Oban–Ardrishaig service profitably if a medium-sized vehicle of about 20 seats was used. The Main Board in London approved purchase of a suitable vehicle the following month as part of an order for three buses, again suggesting that, price and other considerations being equal, the question of placing the order in Scotland be favourably considered. On this occasion the chassis at least were to be 'home built'. Few Albion psvs were ever purchased but these three buses were to be normal control Victors. US 2008-10 had Park Royal bodies with 20 bus seats and a mail compartment at the back. The Oban–Ardrishaig service received its 'winter' bus on 1st October.

At the end of August the year's only other new vehicle arrived, this being of interest on a number of scores. US 2246 was an AEC Regal I fitted with an 8.8 litre oil engine, the first to be tried by the company; the 32-seat coach body was again from Park Royal. Although registered in Glasgow and painted and lettered in full MacBraynes livery, this machine was only on hire, presumably so that experience of the diesel engine could be obtained. From this small beginning a long association, lasting more than 35 years with the products of the Southall factory, was to be forged.

Reverting to April, it had been considered prudent to apply for a licence for a Glasgow to Fort William service via the new road through Glencoe then nearing completion. Similar applications were

made by J Hutton Shields of Kinlochleven and the Kinlochleven Road Transport Company as well as W Alexander & Sons. Several local operators had applied in 1932 for services from Kinlochleven to Tyndrum and Glasgow but these were turned down because the road was nowhere near completion. It was agreed between the two major operators, MacBraynes and Alexanders, that conflict should be avoided; although each application would stand, the Traffic Commissioners were to be advised that a joint service would be operated if licences were granted. Receipts would be divided on a 50-50 basis, each operator working from the appropriate end each morning. When the Traffic Courts sat there were many objections to the various applications and the hearings determined that the matter be decided on the basis of individual applications. The hearing in the Southern Traffic Area occupied five days in early July and in the Northern Area three days in September.

The railway line from Spean Bridge to Fort Augustus via Invergarry had always been in a bad state financially, and the LNER announced complete closure after 1st December 1933, arrangements being made with the Fort William operator, A MacIntyre, to provide a bus service between these points. MacBraynes were concerned that this increase in MacIntyre's service would affect the seasonal tourist traffic on the Caledonian Canal steamers. They applied to extend their Inverness–Fort Augustus service to Fort William and also to operate from Fort Augustus to Spean Bridge, at the same time opposing MacIntyre's application; the hearing took place over three days at the end of Nov-

ember. MacBraynes' application was turned down and the licence granted to MacIntyre and MacRae & Dick of Inverness jointly, each operator to run the service in alternate months. MacBraynes asked their parent railway company, the LMS, to protest to the LNER over use of a non-railway associated company for the replacement service, but to no avail.

Arising from the Traffic Court hearings, a licence was granted around the close of the year to operate the through Glasgow–Fort William service, but only in the summer period between 25th March and 6th October of each year. Shields was granted an all-year-round service from Fort William to Tyndrum, connecting thence with the W Alexander & Sons service from Glasgow to Oban. Only one journey in each direction was permitted on both these services and all tickets were to be interchangeable. The LMS and LNER both raised objection to the granting of the licences but these were overruled by the authorities.

1934 was to prove an eventful year. By January agreement had been reached with J Hutton Shields to take over his business, which, apart from the new service, included an established Kinlochleven to Fort William run. Six vehicles were involved, the purchase price being £2500. Mr Shields was offered employment at a salary of £250 per annum and 3rd April was to see the takeover effected. Of the six vehicles acquired, two were taken into the fleet, these being SB 3874, a 14-seat Bedford WLG coach, new in 1931, and GG 9318, a 1932 Albion Viking 26-seater with Cowieson bus bodywork. The other Shields vehicles were two 14-seat Chevrolets of 1929 and

1931 vintage, a 1929 20-seat Dennis and a 1927 14-seat Beardmore. In 1931 three return journeys were being operated between Kinlochleven and Ballachulish Quarries, and on 5th May 1932 a coordinated timetable with the Kinlochleven Road Transport Co service was introduced, but there is no record of this service being in operation when the firm sold out and it is known that this route became very unprofitable around this time.

No sooner had Shields been acquired than the company was approached by the Kinlochleven Road Transport Company with a view to disposing of their bus service between Ballachulish and Kinlochleven. The Certificate of Fitness on their only bus was due to expire at the end of June and the vehicle needed replacing, but the company had not the cash available to do this. Late in its independent existence the Caledonian Railway had taken a 20% stake in the company at its inception in 1922 as it saw the proposed service as a useful link between the end of the Ballachulish branch line and Kinlochleven, both for passengers and goods. After the grouping, their shares passed to the LNER. MacBraynes duly took over responsibility for the stage service, but not the vehicle, with effect from Sunday, 1st July, £200 being paid for the goodwill, and the Kinlochleven company henceforth concentrated solely on its haulage work.

The following day was to witness the inauguration of the Fort William–Glasgow service via Kinlochleven, Ballachulish, Glencoe and Tyndrum, two return journeys being operated each day, the afternoon runs being connections in and out of Alexanders' Glasgow–Oban service at

Tyndrum. This important new service was to become one of the most prestigious and famous of all MacBraynes' road operations. August 1st heralded the entry into service of two very advanced vehicles specially ordered from AEC in the form of the side-engined Q type fitted with oil engines, Daimler fluid transmission and Wilson preselector gearboxes. These luxurious 32-seat coaches, US 6895/6, had Park Royal bodies, the entrance being immediately behind the front wheels. The engine compartment was insulated from the saloon by a lining of eel grass, a West African plant with peculiar sound-deadening qualities and reported to be very effective. Reminiscent of London's Green Line coaches were the side-mounted roof boards extolling 'Glasgow–Fort William Grand Tour–Loch Lomond, Pass of Glencoe, Loch Leven, Loch Linnie'. A roof mounted luggage compartment was also fitted at the rear. The simplified fleet name 'MACBRAYNES' made its debut on the sides of these fine vehicles; an additional adornment was a small Scottish lion rampant contained in a gold lined square – the traditional ornate gold lining around the side panels being retained as was the 'Royal Route' emblem. On the rear of each coach

A Highland meeting point in 1934. Bus-steamer connections were an important part of Mac-Braynes' daily operations, and in this view at Ardrishaig three of the company's buses are seen meeting the steamer from Glasgow and the Firth of Clyde piers. The two Maudslays awaiting departure for Oban are - nearest to the camera - one of the half-canopy quartet of 1929, next to which stands one of the former normal control vehicles (SB 3367–9) now heavily rebuilt and newly rebodied by Cowieson. Facing towards Tarbert is US 2246, the oil engined AEC Regal hired in 1933 and taken into stock in the following year.

An example of Highland road, rail and steamer coordination at its best was at Fort William where all three forms of transport terminated within a few yards of each other, and it became a major centre for MacBraynes' road motor services. The building to which the list of bus and ship departure times is affixed was demolished in 1935 to make way for MacBraynes' famous modern office, waiting room and bus garage complex which opened in the following year at a cost of £6600. The Bracebridge bodied Bedford awaits departure to Kinlochleven via Ballachulish.

was carried the legend 'MacBraynes For The Highlands' in attractive gold block lettering, a feature which was to become a hallmark of all future MacBrayne vehicles throughout the firm's existence. Strangely, no record appears to survive as to how the decision to purchase Q types was arrived at, but the high cost, £1900.13.6d for each complete vehicle, is recorded. The through-summer service was duly withdrawn, as stipulated by the licence, on 6th October.

In April 1934 authority had been given to order two new vehicles for Fort William area services plus one Bedford chassis suitable for 20-seat bodywork but fitted out as a 14-seater 'sun saloon', to cost approximately £500, for the Inverness to Fort Augustus tour service, and these three vehicles were registered at the same time as the Qs. The sun saloon, US 6894, was a WTB with

Duple body; again, from this small beginning, Duple were to become one of Mac-Braynes' principal body suppliers over the next three decades. US 6892/3 were two further Albion Victors, this time of forward control layout and costing £882.13.9d each. An interesting feature of the Cowieson 20-seat bodies was the cut-away bulkhead behind the driver and the rearmost side cab window angled across the top of the bonnet to enable the bus to be one-man operated. The new fleet name style was used as on the Qs, but in addition the words 'Royal Mail Services' also appeared towards the rear of the sides. Large roof luggage racks were included.

The trials with AEC Regal US 2246 had obviously been judged successful for the vehicle was purchased during 1934, £963 being the price paid; this was possibly the original cost price of the vehicle less the hire charges, which had amounted to around £420. In June a partner was found for it in the form of BMG 358, another 8.8 litre oil engined Regal I Park Royal 32-seat vehicle, this having previously been a de-

monstrator new the previous year. The sum paid was £1150 and it joined its sister vehicle on the demanding Glasgow to Tarbert route with its long twisting climbs to Rest and be Thankful, often at a gradient of 1 in 7.

Rebodying of older chassis became a feature of company policy over the years, starting with SB 3367–9, the 1929 normal control Maudslays which reappeared by the middle of 1934 converted to forward control (this work costing a total of £352.4.6d) and fitted with 32-seat Cowieson bodies. The three bodies cost just under £2000 and represented a worthwhile investment when it is considered that upwards of 12 years further service was given by these buses in their rebuilt form. Disposed of during the year were 1926 Morris-Commercial SB 2698, which departed for further service with Kennedy, Kiltarlity, on 5th March for £30, and similar 1925 vehicles SB 2665/6 which were dismantled for spares.

With these further expansions of services and new bases being established, the matter

The two AEC Q oilers purchased in 1934 for the new Fort William–Glasgow run were impressive looking vehicles, though perhaps not quite as modernistic in appearance as some other operators' vehicles of this type. Compared with some Qs they had a very short front overhang which, combined with the usual set-back rear axle, resulted in a very long wheelbase. It is not recorded how the single rear wheels coped in the adverse road conditions so often encountered in the Highlands in winter, although this problem did not have to be faced in their early years as their Fort William–Glasgow operation was a summer-only one. The front view of US 6896 is taken at the Glencoe crossroads and shows the legend painted on the front indicator glass – 'The Glencoe Route'. The rear view, seen in a coachbuilder's photograph prior to delivery, illustrates well the informative side route boards and the rear legend 'See This Scotland', which was not perpetuated on other vehicles.

of garage accommodation was again given consideration, resulting in approval in July for the erection of a building at Kinlochleven, estimated to cost in the region of £750. On 26th October a special resolution was passed by the Board to seek authority for the company title officially to revert to David MacBrayne Ltd and this was approved by the Registrar of Companies on 8th November, after which date the 'new' title was adopted.

The new year dawned with attempts being made to revise the new Glasgow–Fort William service to operate the summer 'tourist' service from Fort William in the afternoon and from Glasgow in the morning instead of the other way about. Apart from the Glasgow holiday period the through service had not shown much signs of popularity and was not expected to do so until the revised timetable was approved. However, the Traffic Commissioner turned down the application, granting the same licence as in 1934 except that operation would not start until 1st May. The saga continued throughout the year,

including at one stage a plan to introduce day return fares, but strong opposition was mounted by the railways and the plans rejected again; even an appeal to the Ministry of Transport was turned down.

1935 was a quiet year on the new vehicle front, only two arriving, Duple bus bodied Bedford WTLs YS 2611/2 with 20 seats and mail compartments at a price of £677.15.0d each. On the debit side only one vehicle departed, 1928 Morris-Commercial ST 4910, sold to R W Sandison, Hillswick, Shetland, for £29. Meanwhile, negotiations had been taking place with two more operators with a view to MacBraynes taking over their services and in April it was decided that both should be acquired. Some months were to pass before the takeovers took effect as delay was encountered in obtaining Ministry of Transport and Traffic Commissioners' approval to transfer licences. The first was to be the business of A Warren of Ballachulish, purchased at a cost of £2000 (£1000 being for plant and vehicles and the same for goodwill). MacBraynes' minute book records the takeover

date as 15th January 1936. Under the terms of sale, Mr Warren was offered employment with a five year agreement at £200 a year. Stage services were from Ballachulish Ferry via Ballachulish Quarry and Glencoe to Tyndrum and charabancs were used on tours from Ballachulish and Kentallen to Glencoe. Details of only four of the recorded five vehicles are known – the fifth may have been a car. The only vehicle retained as a psv was SB 4036, a 1932 20-seat Waveney bodied Commer Centaur. Thorneycroft SB 3589, being in chassis form only, was converted to a lorry for MacBraynes' haulage operations and Chevrolet SB 3866 and Lancia ES 8505 were sold in the spring of 1936.

The second acquisition was of greater significance in that it would further consolidate the company's position in both the Fort William and Inverness areas. Earlier in the year application had been made to extend the Inverness–Fort Augustus service to Fort William, but this was unsuccessful. The General Manager reported that negotiations had taken place with both

The last Albion buses purchased new by Mac-Braynes were a pair of half-cab petrol engined Victors built in 1934. Although principally intended for stage service operation, with cut-away bulkhead for one-man operation and a mail compartment at the back, they were equipped by Cowieson with 20 very comfortable coach seats which made them suitable for tour work when required.

A MacIntyre, Fort William, and MacRae & Dick Ltd in an attempt to acquire their services. By April 1935 good progress was being made in negotiations with MacIntyre, who had commenced services in 1926 and was now running ten 14-seat Fords. Agreement was reached by June but a long delay followed when MacRae & Dick opposed the application for licences. This led MacBraynes to question 'whether an omnibus company was at liberty to sell the goodwill of their business'. In December the press reported that MacBraynes had again applied to the Commissioners to take over the MacIntyre services, these being Fort William–Inverness, Fort William–Fort Augustus and Spean Bridge–Fort Au-

gustus. The report stated that 'MacBraynes had purchased the services on these routes and negotiated with MacRae & Dick and the County Council re-coordination of timetables and fares'. The application was adjourned for a special sitting of the Commissioners.

Early in 1936 both MacBrayne and MacRae & Dick were advertising services from Inverness to Fort Augustus and Fort William to commence on 21st January. MacBraynes were to operate two throughout journeys southbound on Mondays to Saturdays with three northbound; MacRae & Dick also operated two return journeys daily throughout, although the Sunday timings were different. In addition two short working return journeys from Fort William to Fort Augustus were to operate except on Sundays, being worked on alternate weeks by each operator. £2000 was paid for the stage services of MacIntyre with an additional £1250 for the tours business. These figures were all for goodwill as no vehicles whatsoever were taken over. Additional vehicles to cover service and

tour requirements were expected to cost over £5000. Mr MacIntyre was given employment with the company on a five-year contract at £350 per year. Payment for the tours side of the operations was not made until March and it is probable that MacIntyre continued with the outstanding work whilst MacBraynes set about the task of finding suitable vehicles with which to operate the tours. During the spring six Bedford WLGs were purchased from W Alexander & Sons for £250 each. The vehicles seated 14 passengers in their dual doorway bodies which were built by Alexander Motors of Edinburgh, a firm having no connection with the previous operator of the vehicles, and were of the all-weather style popular in 1931 when they were built. Registration numbers were WG 502/8/11-4.

In January 1936 the MacBraynes Board approved the acquisition of the Corriemony to Inverness service of C A MacDonald of Glenurquart and started running the service in June. Mr MacDonald being engaged at £2 per week for three years. £240

was paid for the business, £100 being for goodwill, £90 for the garage and £50 for the vehicle, Chevrolet ST 5930 of *circa* 1930 vintage. It was not used but disposed of on 1st July for £15. Prior to taking over this operator, MacBraynes had only operated through to Corriemony on two Saturday journeys projected off their daily Glenurquart service.

Six more Duple bodied Bedfords, 20-seat WTB models, formed the new stock intake for 1936. YS 8462/3/5 were the first three to arrive and these had service bus bodies with mail compartments, the complete vehicles being priced at £654.17.6d each. YS 8464/6-8, which were coaches and did not feature mail compartments, cost £680.2.6d each except for one vehicle which, for some unexplained reason, cost £17 extra. These coach bodies were of the current Duple style incorporating a steeply stepped waistrail. They had sliding heads and interior heaters; all subsequent vehicles built up to the end of 1939 were to have these refinements. Roofs were painted red and the fleet name and other insignia were

as seen on the Qs in 1934, but the gold lining-out was dispensed with.

Also in January 1936 the General Manager recommended rebodying of further Maudslay chassis, this time involving SB 3360-3. These bodies would cost £750 each with an estimated £100 being spent on reconditioning the chassis and fitting new cylinder heads to the engines, which had been suffering from cracked exhaust manifolds, a re-design recommended by Maudslay to overcome this problem. The vehicles in their new form were expected to give a minimum of seven years good service and would be an economical way of acquiring modern rolling stock. Thus they received new 31-seat Park Royal coach bodies with cant panels formed of Triplex reinforced glass. These bodies were the forerunners of the company's standard heavy duty coach body for more than a decade. A further change in the livery took place, the mudguards being painted cream and the roofs red. As with the previous rebodied Maudslays good value was to be obtained from these bodies, two lasting nearly 14 years

with the others being transferred to new chassis after the war to give a total of 22 years' service each.

During the summer construction was underway of the fine new garage, offices and waiting rooms alongside the pier, and opposite the railway station, in Fort William, sanction for the building of which had been given in January 1935. The whole project cost £6600. Commencing in July a late return journey left Fort William at 10.50pm on Saturdays for Spean Bridge, operated on alternate weeks by the joint operators. At the end of the summer quarter, 30th September, the company reported an increase of 28,000 passenger journeys over the same period in 1935, 18,000 coming from acquired services and 10,000 from 'our now catering for special party excursion work'; fare receipts for the quarter increased by £4500. Sold towards the end of the year were Morris-Commercial SB 3486 (on 20th October) and the only Leyland in the fleet, former Link Lines' TS2 GE 4586.

The first delivery of new large capacity

A pair of new Duple-bodied 20-seat mail buses were purchased in 1935 on Bedford's WTL goods chassis and they were destined to live their lives out working from Inverness where the second of them is seen on a wet day at the Farraline Park bus stand.

Fort William pier in the summer of 1937 showing the new MacBraynes building on the left and a quartet of buses. In the foreground, from left to right, are GG 9318, the Cowieson-bodied Albion Viking taken over from Shields in 1934, a Park Royal-bodied Albion Victor bought new by Mac-Braynes in 1933 (US 2009), and a year-old Bedford Duple coach YS 8466. Peering out from the background between the two Albions is one of the four Maudslays of 1932 bought for the Glasgow–Ardrishaig run but now relegated to other work.

The new, heavy looking Park Royal coach bodies of 1936 sat rather uncomfortably upon the 1929 Maudslay chassis of SB 3360–3, the overall effect of which was particularly marred by the front mudguards which, in an attempt at streamlining, were built unusually low at the front and projected well ahead of the radiator. However, the four vehicles were destined to give good service in their new guise. These, and all subsequent large vehicles purchased before the war, were fitted with semaphore trafficators.

vehicles for nearly three years took place early in 1937 in the form of three AEC Regals with 32-seat Park Royal coach bodies, registered AGE 828-30. Their service with the company was to be short-lived – in 1940 they were requisitioned by the War Department, never to return. The bodies were similar to those used in rebodying the Maudslays in 1936, but the glass cant panels were not incorporated. Complete, each vehicle cost £1679.11.6d, considerably less than the Qs purchased three years earlier. They were intended for the Glasgow–Tarbert service, displacing SB 4018–21 onto less onerous duties.

Other new arrivals were four Bedford WTBs, all with Duple coach bodies, AYS 373/4 being 25-seat coaches, and AYS 372/5 20-seat saloons with mail compartments. The two coaches had much more pleasantly rounded bodies than their counterparts of a year earlier, having dispensed with the stepped waistrail. The whole batch represented a capital investment of £2750.5.0d.

By the summer of 1937 an additional mail run was being operated on Mondays to Saturdays from Kinlochleven to Tyndrum at the early hour of 5.35am, returning at 7.30am. Fare-paying passengers were carried on this service, but a similar overnight service from Fort William to Kingussie did not cater for passengers.

Early in the year, with an eye to further expansion, the Board proposed that, with improvements being planned for the Glenfinnan to Arisaig road, part of 'the Road to the Isles', application should be made for a licence to serve this route. This was not expected to be granted but it was felt that it would conserve the company's position should the need arise later. An explanation was forwarded to the LNER, setting out the reasons behind the planned application, but at the hearing the railway strongly opposed the idea and, following representations from the County Road Surveyor, the application was withdrawn until the road was completed.

The beautiful Isle of Mull became a focus of attention for MacBraynes in 1937. Licences had been granted to an hotel owner, Mrs MacDonald of Dervaig, in June 1935 for bus services on the island plus excursions and tours. After several unsuccessful attempts and despite opposition from MacBraynes, who feared abstraction from their steamer traffic, Mrs MacDonald eventually obtained licences for services from Dervaig to Craignure via Tobermory and Dervaig to Salen direct, operation commencing on 22nd February. Mac-Braynes had been considering purchase of a motor boat to work an Oban–Craignure

summer service and it was felt desirable to obtain a ROAD SERVICE LICENCE on Mull to link up with this, so the manager was instructed to try to negotiate with Mrs MacDonald to acquire the licences. In October the matter was still under review, loadings being reported as poor with losses of at least £1 per day. Mrs MacDonald had made several changes to her services in an attempt to popularise them but by the end of the year the hotel had been sold and, as there were reported to be no takers for the services, these had been abandoned. As nothing further is recorded concerning the proposed motor boat service one can only

The most stylish and handsome of all MacBraynes coaches of the nineteen-thirties were probably the three AEC Regals delivered early in 1937. Park Royal's coach styling reached its zenith with these vehicles; they were less 'heavy' looking than the rebodied Maudslays of 1936 and were more pleasantly rounded at the rear than the next batch of Regals delivered in 1939.

The full flowering of MacBraynes' livery was reached in 1939 in the beautiful red, green and ivory colour scheme that was to last until the end. The famous MacBraynes Highlander, standing proudly with targe and claymore, also made his appearance for the first time on units of the bus fleet, a particularly unusual feature on this AEC Regal being the Highlander cut-out mounted on the radiator. The wavy white band, presumably representing the sea which was so much a part of MacBraynes' operations and the Highland way of life, was the only livery feature that failed to last.

Three little Bedford 14-seaters on modified goods type WLG chassis were purchased in 1939. Only 14-seaters and weighing less than 2½ tons apiece, they were ideal for touring parties wishing to explore the more inaccessible and difficult areas of Highland terrain. Roll-back canvas centres were fitted to the roofs of their Duple bodies.

Saturday journey on the Fort William–Spean Bridge services was introduced on Wednesdays as well. The start of the summer services also saw the introduction of a new express service operated twice a day between June and September from Ballachulish Station to Tyndrum with a short stop at Glencoe Hotel to enable passengers to take refreshments before continuing their journey through the scenic grandeur of the Pass of Glencoe. This was a joint operation, the service on alternate weeks being provided by Alexander McConnacher of Ballachulish. Although only two return trips were operated, two vehicles were required to maintain the timetable, the departures from Tyndrum being only 15 minutes apart. In the following summer the two journeys were provided only during July and August, a single trip each way sufficing in June and September.

New vehicle deliveries for 1938 were to consist of only two units, BGE 627/8, further Bedford WTBs with Duple 20-seat plus mail compartment bodies, the total purchase price for each vehicle being £693.3.6d. Only one vehicle was disposed of, this being in the last quarter of the year when one of the original Bedfords, SB 3832, was sold.

It was now ten years since the 'new' company had been formed and the government contract was due for renewal. A supplemental agreement for the last two months of 1938 was followed by a new agreement operative from 1st January 1939. The company was to continue all services then in operation, and it was empowered to introduce other services should it see fit to do so. The agreement stipulated, among other things, that mails be conveyed on the Fort William–Glasgow service on Sundays and must also be conveyed on that day between Inverness and Fort William, 'arrangements for such carriage to be made with the joint operator'. The contract also listed the overnight service from Fort William to Kingussie and back, still showing it as 'Mails

assume that MacBraynes had finally decided against introducing it – had they wanted the bus licences they were now virtually theirs for the taking. Over 25 years were to elapse before MacBrayne buses were to be seen on the delightful route from Craignure to Tobermory.

Three vehicles left the fleet during 1937, indirectly replaced by the new Regals. The surviving 1929 Maudslay, ST 5453, departed bringing in the princely sum of £15 and the remaining ex-Link Lines buses, Crossleys GG 1619/20, were sold for £15 and £25 respectively, considerably less than their book value. With the introduction of the winter timetable, changes were made to the days of operation of certain journeys on the Glenurquart and Corriemony service, following the acquisition of the Mac-Donald share of the service the previous year.

From 24th January 1938, at the behest of the Post Office, a mail box was carried on the 4.55pm (6.00pm Saturdays) bus from Ballachulish Ferry to Kinlochleven for the benefit of residents of the few isolated crofts bordering this undulating route along the hillside above the south shore of Loch Leven. From the commencement of the summer timetables in June, the late

The last touring coach delivered to MacBraynes before the outbreak of war was CGE 199, a Duple-bodied Bedford WTB 26-seater with new style radiator. It is seen on a poorly surfaced moorland road some 1400 ft above sea level on a Loch Ness tour from Inverness.

Only'. Vehicle depreciation was to be calculated at a rate of 20% per annum, a figure designed to give a vehicle life of about seven years which was realistic in view of the company's arduous operating terrain.

Before the summer of 1939, eight new vehicles entered service. Four (CGE 199–202) were Bedfords, the first being a 26-seat Duple coach-bodied WTB at £733 which had similar-looking bodywork to the two coaches of 1937 though it differed in detail, whilst the rest were little 14-seat Duple WLGs costing £576.14.7d apiece. These four Bedfords sported the revised radiator grille as fitted to the new O models. CGE 203–6 were more 7.7 AEC Regals with Park Royal coach bodies of the now standard pattern, this time with 35 seats, purchase of which had been sanctioned back in 1937 at a cost of £1701.14.6d per vehicle. Another livery change took place, the result being extremely attractive and tasteful,

reflecting the great pride taken in the appearance of this company's vehicles, a feature sadly lacking today in the majority of major operators' fleets throughout Britain. Roofs, backs and side flashes became pale green, and to the red lower panels were added the now famous 'Highlander'. Two wavy white lines appeared at the base of the sides, presumably intended to indicate the company's connection with the sea, but this particular adornment of the livery was not to last long. One omission, which was thankfully to be short-lived, was that of the 'Royal Route' insignia. Although the nature of the work carried out is unknown, nearly £400 was spent in 1939 on reconstructing both the AEC Qs, US 6895/6.

In January the Board heard that the business and properties of A & J MacPherson of Fort William were for sale. It realised that the acquisition of this operator would eliminate further competition to their tour operations and bus services and establish MacBraynes as the principal operator in the Fort William area. The additional work could be undertaken with little addition to plant. Negotiations were commenced and, in April, purchase was approved. Included in the deal was the garage

and a fleet of taxis, but neither of these were of interest to the company and arrangements were made to sell this part of the business to MacRae & Dick for £2052. The bus and coach services were taken over from 1st July, the excursions being incorporated within the existing MacBraynes programme. Of the four stage services involved, two were of a rural nature. The Achnacarry service had been taken over from R Campbell in May 1936 and consisted of two return journeys on Tuesdays, Thursdays and Saturdays, with a further late run on Saturdays. By October 1937 Tuesday and Thursday operations had changed to Wednesday and Friday. Two journeys each way were operated on the first Sunday in the month, but they survived barely a year after MacBraynes took over. The second was a twice daily – including Sundays – route to Glenfinnan. MacPherson was granted a licence for this service, which opened on 11th October 1937 with much local pomp and ceremony, despite opposition from the LNER and MacBraynes, and stated at the time that he 'hoped to extend to Mallaig when the road was suitable'. The busiest and most important service acquired was that to Corpach,

and Campbeltown both for freight and passengers. Since March 1937 MacBraynes had been sole owners of this fleet and in 1938 had asked the government to include this route in its contract for subsidised services, but to no avail. Thus, in April 1939 the Board resolved to abandon the service; in August they publicised their intention of withdrawing these steamers at the end of September and transferring cargo to road haulage. To cater for displaced passenger traffic, MacBraynes applied for a licence to extend their Glasgow–Tarbert service to Campbeltown. This resulted in a counter-application from West Coast Motor Services of Campbeltown for a Monday to Saturday service, thence to Glasgow. Withdrawal of the steamer was subsequently delayed until 14th March 1940, but nevertheless, having obtained their licence, MacBraynes inaugurated the once daily through passenger service to Campbeltown on 2nd October.

A very gloomy threat hung over the whole United Kingdom during the summer of 1939, the danger of another war with Germany. The situation worsened as the summer wore on, and from mid-August a marked fall-away in the number of passengers was apparent as people made for home or cancelled holidays, so that by the end of the month traffic had dwindled almost to winter levels. Late in the month it was agreed that tourist orientated services be suspended after 2nd September, not a day too soon as things were to turn out. With the outbreak of war on 3rd September, plans were soon made for more reductions in certain services from October when normal winter schedules were due to commence. The trunk services to Glasgow maintained the normal basic winter frequency of past years, with some slight retimings, but many rural services had one or more journeys deleted. A 25% cut was made on the Corpach route, although it is probable that larger capacity vehicles were now in operation thereon. The company assisted with the transport of evacuees from Glasgow during the early days of the war.

In eleven years MacBraynes had built up a substantial fleet of vehicles and a large network of road passenger services in the scenic West Highlands. Passenger carryings by road had risen from 116,929 in 1930 to 254,295 in 1933 and to 482,071 in 1938. No one could know how long the war was to last, but to MacBraynes, along with most other bus operators, it would inevitably bring problems with changed patterns of demand for bus and coach services, and a dramatic increase in passenger journeys, particularly by servicemen going to and from leave.

this being of a more local nature. It had been MacPherson's original service, although until about 1935 operation was shared with another local firm, Cruickshank & Clarke who were subsequently acquired. Up to sixteen journeys each way were operated on weekdays, with seven on Sundays. Since 1st March 1937 several weekday journeys had been diverted via Inverlochy Village. This route was to become the busiest and most frequent of all MacBraynes services, and over much of the next thirty years vehicles with bus-type bodywork were purchased especially for local work in and around Fort William. The fourth ex-MacPherson operation was a works service to the British Aluminium factory.

Ten psv's came with the business, but only two were retained, those being ST 9172, a 1937 14-seat Guy Wolf, and ST 9188, a normal control Albion with a 14-seat Cadogan body, also new in 1937. Of the others, WG 501 was a Bedford WLG from the same source as those purchased by MacBraynes in 1936. MS 8265 was an Albion, new in 1928, and VA 9856 another Albion of 1930 vintage. Other Albions were VA 4923, DV 1242, WG 1511; the

remaining two vehicles were of Morris manufacture, SB 4034 dating from 1932 and SL 1451. These last five vehicles had a total book value of only £110. Apart from ST 9172 and ST 9188 it is doubtful if any of the others were used by MacBraynes as by the 19th July disposal of these eight had been sanctioned, and by the end of the year all had been sold, realising the grand sum of £75! Goodwill for the business was valued at £1118, the vehicles at £825 and an office in the High Street, which was taken over, at £255.

A number of vehicles left the fleet during the year. In April, Morris-Commercial SB 3484 of 1929 departed, in June the remaining 1931 Bedford WLB, SB 3833, was sold and July saw another Morris-Commercial, SB 3485, sold to the Fort William Faith Mission for £12.10.0d. As previously mentioned, towards the end of the year eight former MacPherson vehicles left, as did SB 3874, the ex-Shields. Bedford WHG of 1931, with Morris-Commercial SB 3487 (the last of the batch) and Bedford WLGs WG 511/4 becoming MacBraynes lorries.

The Clyde & Campbeltown Shipping Company had, for many years, operated two or three steamers between Glasgow

Alan Nightingale's article covers a small, though very interesting, portion of the overall history of one of Scotland's major bus operators. It forms part of a much larger complete history of the company's sixty-five years of bus operation which is now in an advanced stage of preparation and will be published as a separate volume in due course. If this article encourages any of our readers to submit information or, especially, photographs which they think may be of value for the complete volume, these will be received (via the Editor) with gratitude.

THE WHEELS MUST KEEP TURNING

Every major operator has adequate and well-equipped workshop facilities providing for maintenance and overhaul works. Such facilities are essential to a well-run fleet, for if revenue is to be earned the wheels must keep turning. However, buses seem to be seldom photographed undergoing repair, perhaps because in this situation they are less glamorous than when earning their keep on the public highway. Repair and maintenance work being carried out by a few South Coast operators is seen in these photographs.

Brighton Hove & District was long renowned for the very extensive body rebuilds carried out in its Hove workshops as a result of which vehicles were often completely transformed in appearance. Vehicles of another Tilling subsidiary, Westcliff-on-Sea, were also dealt with as well as BH&B's own.

A typical Brighton bus is this Tilling type open staircase Regent. It is seen in wartime grey paint bearing the fleet name Crosville with whom it was one of very many buses on wartime loan from various operators; at the war's end it was purchased by them. Windowless and ready to have its body dismantled, it has returned to Hove for reconditioning, whence it will return to Crosville service carrying an ECW body. In front stands a later BH&D bus, temporarily staircaseless.

Portslade has long been renowned as the huge and well-equipped main works of Southdown, whose beautiful green liveried buses were always such a splendid sight until overtaken by the dull anonymity of NBC corporate livery. In this early thirties view, three of the company's once numerous fleet of Leyland TDls are seen undergoing repair in the body shops. These three have low-height Leyland bodies and are part of a fleet of 36 such vehicles purchased in 1930 and withdrawn eight years later. No 854, nearest the camera, finished its working life with Rothesay Tramways.

The washing bay at Maidstone & District's Gillingham depot in the days before labour saving washing machines came into existence. Receiving attention from no fewer than four washers is a newly delivered Leyland Titan of 1935 vintage. Maidstone & District once operated many of these characterful vehicles which were torque convertor equipped until just after the war. Many of the company's pre-war Titans and Tigers provided a useful source of supply of mechanical components for Beadle-built coaches of the 1950s.

The Second World War brought enforced neglect to many vehicles, and once peace was restored many operators embarked on programmes of heavy reconstruction. East Kent's main body shops at Canterbury were destroyed by bombing and most major work had to be transferred to Faversham where a Dennis Ace is seen receiving attention. Dating from 1934, this vehicle would ordinarily have been scrapped by 1946 when this photograph was taken, but the war extended the lives of many vehicles including this one. Its East Kent-built body is seen receiving major attention which made it good for another three years service.

Southern Vectis was once renowned for its fleet of Dennises. Two of the last are seen awaiting routine maintenance on the pits in the bright, airy docking area at the company's Newport garage in 1958. The Dennis Ace - one of the last of its type in public service anywhere in Britain - was one of a pair of Harrington-bodied 20-seaters purchased in 1936; it had only a few weeks service left. The Duple-bodied Lancet, eleven years its junior, was acquired with the fleet of Nash's Luxury Coaches of Ventnor in 1956 and later saw service in the Canary Islands after being withdrawn by Southern Vectis in 1959.

SINGLE DECKERS OF THE LGOC

Bus operation in London has always been best renowned for being worked predominantly by double deckers, and some very famous types of bus have been produced over the years. Single deck operations have, in contrast, been rather in the background although the role they have played has varied in significance from time to time. In this review, GEORGE ROBBINS details the various types of single deckers operated by the London General Omnibus Company between 1912 and 1933.

ALTHOUGH motor buses have been running in London more or less regularly since 1904, for many years all were double deck for few operators could afford to run a single deck vehicle with its much reduced seating capacity. London's double deck buses were, to some extent, standard, being 34-seaters (16 passengers inside and 18 outside on the open top deck) and it was possible to work these vehicles on all central London routes. Strict weight limits set by the Metropolitan Police prevented any departure from this seating capacity.

In the very early years there had been several single deck workings, including those in 1904 by Pioneer, in

Single deck operation by the New Central Omnibus Company came about because of a height restriction at Long Ditton on the Kingston–Esher run. The company standardised on Leylands, and one of the two replacement vehicles of 1912 is seen here waiting to depart for Kingston. It was less than a year old when control of Central passed to General. The swivel destination boards front and rear are of interest.

B 1879 was one of the nine original LGOC single deckers of 1912 which inaugurated the motor bus service through Blackwall Tunnel. These 16-seaters quickly proved popular and before long the frequency of the service was doubled. In the second view the same bus is seen plunging into the depths of the tunnel at its southern end. The cobblestones must have made the gradient difficult to negotiate with the narrow tyres of the day when the surface was wet or greasy.

The prototype 20-seat single decker is seen at work on route 79 in place of a Central Leyland. The year is 1914 and it carries a so-called bentwood-type body incorporating curved pillars to give greater width internally. It was for a while a special private hire coach (see *VINTAGE BUS ANNUAL NO 1*, page 52).

1908 by Pullman, and others. But they had all been very short-lived and it was not until late in 1911 that the first single deck operation of a permanent nature commenced. This was by the New Central Omnibus Company Ltd, who had taken over a horse bus service between Kingston and Esher. This ran under a low railway bridge at Long Ditton and although a double deck horse bus could negotiate this archway, a double deck motor bus could not. New Central, therefore, converted two of their older Leyland motor buses into single deckers. Only one bus was required to operate the hourly service on this short route which took only 24 minutes, the second bus being a spare. Two new single deck Leylands to an improved style were introduced in 1912. The operation of New Central was undertaken by the London General Omnibus Company from January 1913 when the Esher route was allotted service number 79. More buses were added to it later in 1913 when the service was increased to run every 15 minutes, the single deckers working from Central's Kingston garage.

During 1912 the few remaining horse bus services in London were rapidly being replaced by motor buses. One of these was that operated by Thomas Tilling Ltd through Blackwall Tunnel. The LGOC replaced this by a new motor bus service 69 which ran from Poplar through the tunnel and on to *The Plume of Feathers* at Plumstead. Here again, although double deck horse buses could work through the tunnel, double deck motor buses could not so the LGOC provided nine new single deck buses for this route and these were sent to the company's Athol Street, Poplar (C) garage. They were, in fact, only the lower deck of a normal bus with an open platform at the back and merely seated sixteen passengers. The nine buses were B 1817, 1828, 1876, 1879, 1881, 1918, 1919, 1925 and 1927. By April 1913 the service was increased from a 10 to a 5-minute headway following the arrival of another nine single deck buses. The full fleet of 19 ran for only two months, for in June the 69 was shortened to

work only between Poplar and Greenwich, reducing the single deck requirement back to nine, the older ones being rebuilt as double deckers.

A prototype body for a new 20-seat single decker was designed early in 1913. This had a wider bentwood-style body enabling some of the passengers to sit facing forwards whereas all seats had been placed longitudinally in the older type of bus. This body was mounted onto a former private hire bus B 1394 which was transferred to the service fleet in September 1913 and presumably then put onto the Esher route. Thirty new single deck buses were built in 1914 with the same style of body and were numbered B 2679–2708. They first worked on route 69, which was re-numbered 108 in March 1914 and extended at each end to work from Bow Road Station to Blackheath. Others were later put onto three new routes:

111 Finsbury Park Station and Muswell Hill Broadway working from Holloway (J) garage; a route which climbed steep hills.

112 Penge and Bromley, a route passing under low railway bridges.

113 Beckenham and Park Langley – one bus under contract to serve a new housing estate. Both 112 and 113 ran from the new garage at Catford, at that time with code letters AN.

These thirty 20-seat bentwood-style buses had been constructed at a time when war appeared imminent and they were designed so that they could be easily converted for use as ambulances. They were taken by the War Department on 1st August 1914 and this had an immediate and drastic effect on all single deck services as only ten vehicles remained available, nine 16-seaters and the prototype 20-seater B 1394. Four were needed for a shortened 108 route working only between Poplar and Greenwich. 111 was curtailed and the service decreased, route 112 was withdrawn, but the 113 lingered on for a few months as it needed only one bus. B 1394 remained for use on route 79 which became an hourly service once more.

War conditions quickly brought a need for more single deck buses in certain areas to carry essential war workers, so a number of double deckers were cut down and became 16-seaters. By mid-1915 more buses went to Holloway garage for route 111 and also opened up a new single deck route 41 (Muswell Hill and Crouch End, later extended to Wood Green). By 1916 many more were needed to carry munitions workers to Woolwich Arsenal and four new single deck routes were planned which were covered by a government subsidy. Another 30 new 20-seat bentwood-style single deck buses were built, these being numbered B 3474–3503. The new routes were:

99 Poplar and Erith via Blackwall Tunnel

99A Poplar and Crayford

109 Penge and Woolwich

110 Farnborough and Crayford

Ten of the new single deckers were ready in time for route 99 to commence on 1st May 1916, but unfortunately the Erith police refused to license the new vehicles on account of their increased width. The LGOC were therefore obliged to work a curtailed service between Woolwich and Erith with charabancs and older buses for two months until the police at last gave way. The route was extended to Poplar on 14th August when the other three services also began. Routes 99 and 99A were worked from Athol Street garage and the others from Streatham (AK). The 110 did not last long but the others continued until the war was over and munitions work ceased, whereupon the government subsidy was withdrawn and the three routes taken off early in April 1919. This enabled the 20-seat bentwood buses to replace the older 16-seaters on routes 111 and 41.

Four of the 20-seaters taken by the War Department in August 1914 came back to the LGOC and a further ten new bodies were built to the bentwood design. These were used on route 108 and on a revival of route 109 between Penge and Bromley from 17th September 1919. By July 1920 the 99 also re-

The wartime B type single deckers perpetuated the same general design as their pre-war ancestors. B 3484 was one of the 1916 batch of thirty built principally to serve the Woolwich Arsenal, but by 1919 – when it was photographed – it had strayed to more countrylike pastures.

Enclosed rear platforms made their appearance in December 1920 on a straight-sided body which differed considerably from the more curvaceous bentwood type. The rather boxy appearance is demonstrated by B 925 as it waits on route 104 at Golders Green Station.

favour of two new services, 61 to Chertsey and 62 to Shepperton. Between September 1921 and May 1922 a further twenty-five 26-seaters were licensed, once again mounted on former double deck B type chassis. As a result, six more new routes commenced: 93 (Uxbridge and Hounslow), 71 (Lewisham and Croydon), 87 (Streatham and Purley), 55 (Acton and Chiswick), 104 (Golders Green and Mill Hill) and 110 (Golders Green and Finsbury Park). At the same time the wartime 99A was reinstated, running now between Woolwich and Crayford. The LGOC provided National with 12 of these 26-seat buses for operation on its behalf in the Watford area and on other country routes north of London. Newer style bodies were subsequently provided for the Muswell Hill routes 41 and 111, similar in appearance to the 26-seaters but limited to 20 seats and with an open platform at the back so as to reduce their weight. Between 1922 and 1924 these gradually replaced the older bentwood buses on the two routes in question.

Although new double deck K and S type buses had been in use in London since 1920, all single deck work was still being undertaken by the B type vehicles. However, in April 1922 a new single deck S type was licensed. This bus, S 265, had a 32-seat body and was sent to Kingston for trials on route 115. A production batch of 24 new single deck S types, carrying a re-designed 30-seat body, entered service between September and November 1922, whilst a further 24 were licensed between April and August 1923. In addition, 15 identical buses were supplied to National for country use. The S type replaced the Bs on routes 55, 79, 87, 108 and 115. Athol Street garage was given a larger supply of the new buses in order to improve the service through the Blackwall Tunnel, and in November 1922 the 108 was joined by a 108A working between Clapton and Lewisham (later extended to Forest Hill).

Notwithstanding the introduction of the S type single deckers, some 110 of the B type continued to work many of the London routes until they were eventually replaced between 1925 and 1927. Meanwhile, however, there had been some changes, the 71 and 93 having been withdrawn and route 55 converted to double deck operation. The

turned, working between Woolwich and Erith.

In December 1920 the LGOC introduced a new type of single deck bus body which, although mounted on a B type chassis, had a wider straightsided body not unlike the lower deck of the standard K type double decker. It had an enclosed platform which enabled the seating capacity to be increased to twenty-six. The prototype was put onto the chassis of B 4900 and it ran on route 99 from Plumstead (AM) garage. Following the success of this bus, 61 more 26-seaters were built, all mounted onto B type chassis which had previously been double deckers. These entered service between February and May 1921 replacing the 16 and 20-seat buses on all six single deck routes. On 20th July 1921 the older 20-seat bentwood buses had to be put back on the 41 and 111 services as the new 26-seat vehicles were found to exceed the weight limit on the railway bridges over the GNR line in Crouch Hill and Crouch End Hill, and this

made a number of 26-seat vehicles surplus. Up to this time single deck buses were found at only six London garages: two in North London – Holloway (J) and Tottenham (AR) for 41 and 111; one in East London – Athol Street (C); and three in South London – Plumstead (AM), Streatham (AK) and Chelverton Road, Putney (AF). The latter had only two B type single decks for the Esher route (79) which had by now been extended to Church Cobham.

In July 1921 fourteen of the surplus buses were sent to Chelverton Road garage to enable new services to be commenced in the Kingston area. These were: 112 (Kingston and Weybridge) and 115 (Kingston and Guildford). Another followed in September 1921, this being 113 (Kingston and Lower Kingswood). At the same time route 79 was further extended to Byfleet. All the single deckers from Chelverton Road were sent to a new garage which opened at Kingston (K) on 4th January 1922. The 112 disappeared in

The single deckers for Muswell Hill were restricted to a capacity of 20 seats and even those built with the new straight-sided body in 1922–4 had open rear platforms as exemplified by B 1317.

Pneumatics were fitted to all the S type single deckers in 1928 and considerably modernised their appearance besides making them immeasurably more comfortable to ride in. The nearside and rear views of these characterful buses are seen on S 433 and S 386 respectively.

replacement for the remaining obsolete B types was the K type single decker. This was introduced as a 24-seater with a new style of body and was the first LGOC passenger vehicle fitted with pneumatic tyres. A rather attractive body was provided, somewhat smaller than the S type, and its smaller wheels made for a lower bus needing only two steps for the passengers to mount as opposed to the three on S types. A unique feature was the use of route number stencils in the top corners of the windows on each side of the front bulkhead. A total of 24 en-

The arrival of the S type represented a big step forward after the rather primitive Bs and gave a very useful increase in carrying capacity. S 439 is seen in its original condition with solid tyres in this quiet suburban scene on route 113.

tered service between August 1925 and January 1926, and were completely new vehicles numbered K 1078–1101. The first six were sent to Hounslow (AV) garage for two new operations, a short route using number 81 between Hounslow and Langley Village and a longer one, 162, between Burnham Beeches, Slough and Staines. The latter was subsequently extended to Leatherhead. Three were sent to National but returned to the LGOC fleet in 1927 where they were always recognisable by their 'RO' Hertfordshire registration numbers. Two were not fitted with pneumatics but had solid tyres and only 20 seats, being intended for trial on the Muswell Hill routes to see if they were suitable for use on the steep hills. Like the B types in use on hilly routes, they were fitted with sprag gear which had to be engaged when descending steep gradients. The rest of the Ks were in use in the Kingston area.

Between 1926 and 1928 another 115 single deck bodies were built, but this time they were mounted on older K type chassis, displacing the double deck bodies that they had formerly carried. Amongst them were certain variations. A further 47 with 20-seat bodies and solid tyres were needed to replace the rest of the B types on the hilly Muswell Hill routes and 26 had solid tyres but were 24-seaters for the other hilly routes such as 99, 104 and 110. Twenty had yet another variation, a 22-seat body and pneumatic tyres. These were painted silver at first, being used as feeder services upon the opening of the extension of the Northern Line of the Underground to Morden in 1926. Five new services inaugurated that spectacular opening on Monday, 13th September 1926, all working from Morden Station forecourt. They were 155 to Worcester Park, 156 to Cheam, 157 to Wallington, 164 to Burgh Heath and 165 to Banstead. Three of the routes had actually commenced in July working from Wimbledon Station. Trade built up so rapidly that routes 156, 157 and 165 were very soon con-

verted to double deck operation. Eleven 24-seaters with pneumatic tyres went for a time to National and East Surrey though most returned to the LGOC eventually. Lastly, in 1928, eleven K types were fitted with larger single deck bodies capable of accommodating 30 passengers.

These new K type saloons had rapidly replaced all the remaining B types which were then withdrawn, and more new single deck services were introduced in addition to those already mentioned. February 1926 saw the commencement of route 154 (Finsbury Park Station and Muswell Hill via Ferme Park Road). In April 1927 came route G1 – operating outside the Metropolitan Police Area between Collier Row and Cranham – followed in November 1927 by 602 (Muswell Hill and

Full-depth sliding windows had been introduced on the S type and were prepetuated on the Ks. These vehicles were far from beautiful when viewed side-on. K 1079 was another of the original Hounslow batch.

Solid tyres were insisted upon by the Metropolitan Police for the B type replacements on the Muswell Hill routes and the seating capacity was kept down to the same low figure of twenty. K 1066 was one such vehicle.

The silver liveried Underground feeders for the opening of the Morden extension in September 1926 were a good publicity stunt and helped to make the opening a great success. K 388 was photographed on the first day, terminating at Banstead.

Edmonton) and 141 (Edgware Station and Borehamwood). April 1928 saw the start of 171 (Kingston and Chertsey) on which there was a weight restriction which led to the vehicles being reduced to 20-seaters. April 1929 saw the introduction of a circular service from Peckham to Ivydale Road and back under route no 621, and of routes G2 and G3 in the Romford area which had to be later renumbered as 187 and 188 when extended to Chadwell Heath in the Met Area. In 1930 a new 209 service commenced to Forest Hill and Eltham.

Mention has been made of route 109 and its revival in 1919 between Penge and Bromley. It was soon extended to Chislehurst and, for a time, from Penge to Forest Hill, but from January 1924 it settled down to operate between Penge and Chislehurst. It was worked by ten 26-seat B types, but LGOC had no garage adjacent to the route and thus had to endure long gar-

K 688 demonstrated various differences in body-work between the small batch of 30-seaters built in 1928 and their predecessors, notably the use of more conventional window-pillar spacings and the fitting of full-drops instead of sliding ventilators.

The petrol electrics operated by Thomas Tilling from its Bromley garage on behalf of the LGOC started life in 1924 on solid tyres and bearing General livery. The official rear view study of XW 9890 shows its original condition whilst XW 9891 is seen at Penge in its final form.

age journeys to and from either Streatham or Nunhead. In 1924 the LGOC handed the route and its ten B type buses to Thomas Tilling to operate from their Bromley (TB) garage. In order to replace the B type, LGOC purchased twelve Tilling-Stevens TS 7 petrol electric chassis for which Tillings built 30-seat single deck bodies, and these went into service in October 1925. At first they carried the General fleet name but this was later replaced by Tilling's own name. Although all were built with solid tyres they were fitted with pneumatics in 1929.

In October 1927 the main section of the Blackwall Tunnel service 108 was converted to double deck operation using specially designed NS types, but owing to low bridges the northern section between Bromley-by-Bow and Clapton still required single deckers and this was numbered 108D. During 1928 all the S type saloons were fitted with pneumatics.

There had been intense competition in London since 1922 between the LGOC and its associated companies and the growing number of independent operators. At first these all ran double deckers but in May 1925 one company, Admiral, introduced a new type of single deck bus to London. This was a Dennis $2\frac{1}{2}$ ton 45hp bus seating 26 passengers. It was, in fact, the first to have pneumatic tyres and preceded by three months the introduction by LGOC of this refinement on K 1078. Some six of these single deck buses were soon ready and they ran on a new route 280 (Finsbury Park Station and Enfield). Redburns Motor Services also bought six similar Dennises, putting two on the 280, so that by March 1926 the route was extended to work between Stroud Green and Forty Hill as 538. In the meantime, Redburns had run their other buses on another new single deck service 551, between Whetstone and Edmonton (Sparklets Works). The LGOC also placed three of their K type buses with pneumatics on this route which soon became quite a popular service as other independent companies such as H M Merry, Biss Bros and Sear Bros, having obtained similar single deck buses, joined in.

In October 1926, Admiral introduced another new saloon bus to London, the first to have four-wheeled

The reversion to the older K type for the 1925 batch of single deckers came as a surprise. They were completely new vehicles with a much lower appearance than the S types due to their more rounded roof and the omission of the upper row of windows. K 1081, one of the original batch of 24, operates from Hounslow garage on the Burnham Beeches-Staines run.

brakes. It was a forward control Dennis E type seating 30 passengers and it also ran on 538. By the end of June 1927 a total of 75 single deck independent buses on pneumatics were working on six routes, mainly in the north of London. Apart from two Maudslays, all were Dennises, 55 being of the $2\frac{1}{2}$ ton normal control model seating 25 or 26 passengers and 28 on the later E type 30-seaters. They ran the following routes:

201 Stroud Green and Edmonton, Sparklets Works 6 buses (Admiral)

263 Finsbury Park Stn and Leyton/ Chingford 15 buses (Aro, Havelock, H H Clench, Fallowfield & Knight)

297 Tufnell Park and King's Cross 4 buses (Clarendon, P H R Harris)

538 Stroud Green and Forty Hill 17 buses (Admiral, Redburns)

550 Finsbury Park and Islington 6 buses (Orange)

551 Whetstone & Edmonton, Sparklets Works 18 buses (Redburns, Biss Bros, Sear Bros, Silver Star, Prince, Uneedus and Skylark)

In November 1926 Redburns were taken over by the LGOC although the

vehicles still retained their old fleet name. Then in May 1927 came the acquisition of Orange followed later in the year by the replacement of the ex-Orange vehicles by double deckers. LGOC also took over Uneedus and Silver Star.

Admiral provided the nucleus for a new concern, the London Public Omnibus Company Ltd, which was registered on 2nd July 1927 and acquired many of the London independents, eventually building up a fleet of over 200. Public acquired all but one of the remaining single deckers operated on the six routes already described, the exception being Prince which continued until taken over by London Transport in 1934. These fleets passed to Public between July and September 1927 except for Sear Bros who lasted out until May 1928. Type letters were allotted by Public to the Dennis buses, the small normal control vehicles becoming DS types whilst the 30-seaters became DEs. An exchange of duties with the LGOC in May 1928 resulted in Public taking over the LGOC duties on routes 538 and 551 which operated henceforth from the Public garages at West Green (WG) and Enfield (E). In another exchange, in February 1929, the LGOC took over 263 and 297 from Public in exchange for the 154 and certain double deck operations. The LGOC ran the 263 from Tottenham (AR) and Leyton (T) garages and the 297 from Holloway (J), but due to a shortage of saloons they borrowed ten Public DS types for a time. Though these retained their blue Public livery, the fleet name was changed by attach-

General's policy of buying up as many of the independent operators as possible brought a number of Dennis E types into the fleet. This Strachan & Brown-bodied 30-seater operated by Mason Brothers of Palmers Green in their Uneedus fleet became D64 in the General numbering scheme when taken over in July 1927.

The exchange of services in May 1928 required General to borrow a number of Dennis 2½ ton single deckers from its subsidiary, Public, to fulfil its operating commitments and these ran in blue livery but carrying the General fleet name on red boards. Public's DS19 of 1925 vintage originated with H M Merry Motor Transport Services Ltd of King's Cross.

The winding-up of Public in December 1929 saw the repainting of its Dennis single deckers in General livery. A one-time Admiral single decker of A T Bennett & Co Ltd of West Green stands at Enfield with a National double decker bringing up the rear.

ing a board with the name 'General' on the sides. A new route had been commenced by Public on 26th November 1928 under the number 204 between Gordon Hill and Tottenham (White Hart Lane). Owing to weight restrictions, four DS types had to be converted to 20-seaters and these buses were destined to continue in service right through to 1936. The London Public Omnibus Co Ltd, which was a General subsidiary, was finally absorbed by its parent company in December 1929.

Following the Public takeover, the LGOC found itself operating some 40 single deck routes with an ageing fleet of non-standard saloon buses of varying seating capacities. This fleet comprised the S type dating from 1922, the K type rebuilds from 1925 and the Dennis buses which they had acquired. A newer type of single deck bus was urgently needed and General took advantage of the developments made by AEC in producing new and improved passenger chassis by ordering a batch of the new Regal 662 model. For these Chiswick built 49 attractive 30-seat rear-entrance bodies. They were numbered T 1–37/39–50 and – with the exception of five transferred to East Surrey – they were soon rebuilt with front entrances.

The first ten of these new buses were sent to Romford (RD) garage on 3rd December 1929 in order to replace the K types on routes G1, G5 and 187. In mid-December 13 T types went to Cricklewood (W) garage for route 104. At the end of the year, eight new Ts were sent to Nunhead (AH) for the Nunhead circular service 621, then three went to Plumstead (AM) garage for route 99C (Erith and Crayford – the main part of the 99 route between Woolwich and Erith having been double decked some years earlier). Although allocated to Plumstead, the 99C was worked from a small garage at Crayford and this, together with the

99C route and the five T types mentioned earlier, were transferred to East Surrey in April 1931. By the beginning of January 1930 ten buses were at Holloway (J) garage for route 110 whilst the remainder were sent to Sutton (A) for 113. The missing number in the series, T38, was a chassis used as a prototype for a fleet of new express

coaches which later developed into the Green Line fleet. To bring the fleet of T type buses up to a round figure of 50, T156 was built and joined the others at Nunhead in July 1930. Though closely resembling them, it carried a front entrance from new.

Passengers must have noticed a great improvement in the luxurious

LS6 was an impressive and forceful-looking Associated Daimler which did not operate as satisfactorily as its owners had hoped. Long associated with Cricklewood garage, it is working therefrom at Golders Green after a windscreen has been fitted to provide a semblance of driver comfort.

The T type was refreshingly modern and handsome, and the performance obtained from its AEC Regal chassis was vastly better than anything that had gone before. T27 is seen at Peckham Rye on the Nunhead circular service 621 early in its life. The cut-away rear end, which was a short-lived feature on most of the class, is seen in the officially posed photograph of T41.

able chassis so an order was placed with Dennis for twenty of their small six cylinder Dart types for which LGOC built suitable bodies. They were 7ft 2ins wide with accommodation for 18 passengers on longitudinal seats and had a front entrance. It should be noted that at the time one-man operation was limited to buses with not more than twenty seats. The first six of this new DA class went to Uxbridge (UX) garage in June 1930 when they replaced 24-seat crew-operated K types on routes 505 (Uxbridge and Ritchings Park) and 506 (Uxbridge and Staines) and later on a new service 507 (Uxbridge and Windsor). DA 7–10 replaced K types on the long 162B between Slough and Leatherhead, the service which, it will be recalled, had the first of the new K type vehicles in 1925. DA 11–20 were also used to replace K types on various routes, including 195 (Chislehurst and Sidcup Station), worked by Sidcup (SP) garage, and they also went to Harrow Weald (HD), where they replaced S types on 353 (North Harrow and Pinner). In December 1931 the G1 at Romford was double decked but the short tail end section between Upminster and Cranham still needed single deckers, so DAs were used for the new G3 service, which this section became.

Between January and April 1931 a further twelve Darts were licensed and many of these were used to open up new routes which subsequently developed and then needed larger vehicles. The first of these was 105, a Hounslow local route which was later extended to Hanworth and Teddington, after which 30-seat S types replaced the Darts. Another route started with Darts was 226 (Golders Green and Cricklewood via Pennine Drive) and this passed to crew-operated T types in 1933. Darts replaced a double deck route in June 1932 when 137 was put on between Hounslow and Chertsey replacing route 90, which was the last home of the double deck K type. Further Dennis Darts were added to the fleet in December 1932 and also in 1933.

One of a small batch of six-wheeled buses introduced by the LGOC in 1928

comfort of the new buses which, on routes 99C, 104 and 110, replaced the older solid-tyred 24-seat K types which for some years had negotiated the steep hills on these particular routes. These Ks, together with a number of pneumatic tyred ones, were then taken out of service.

Whilst the LGOC was contemplating improved buses for the main single deck services in London, they also had in mind a different venture which was initiated in 1929 and eventually came to fruition in 1930. This was the introduction of small capacity buses which could be one-man operated and used on certain routes with limited passenger potential. AEC did not build a suit-

Dennis's Dart chassis did not prove particularly popular with operators except for the LGOC who purchased 42 of them for one-man operation on quieter routes. DA38 was one of the final batch put into service in the first quarter of 1931.

The second batch of LTs differed from their predecessors in having a rear destination blind display instead of relying on slip boards as demonstrated by LT 1136. The rear bumpers and the glass window louvres were short-lived features.

The Chiswick-built Ts and their six-wheeled double deck counterparts which were numbered in the LT class carried radiators which must have ranked amongst the ugliest ever produced. Their performance in service was not too good either! T 1001 appears to have lost the innards from its nearside headlamp.

was a single decker, LS6, the only one of a class of otherwise rather large double deckers. This spent all its working life on route 104 from Cricklewood garage. LS6 had petrol electric transmission but, in common with the rest of its class, it was not a success. It was an altogether different type of six-wheeler that General found most suitable for the replacement of the bulk of its single deck buses. It employed the AEC 664 type Renown chassis which was chosen so that a high capacity 35-seat front entrance body could be built. The first one, LT 1001, was licensed on 24th January 1931 at Hendon garage for trials on route 104. Another 49 of the same type were put onto the road in April 1931, numbered LT 1002–50. Twenty-six of these (including LT 1001) went to Muswell Hill garage to replace the 20-seat K types on route 111, the other 24 being sent to Holloway for routes 41A and 110. It should be noted that from 1927 the 41 route had been worked in two sections, on which only the section between Muswell Hill and Crouch End Broadway needed single deckers. In April 1930 it was reduced further and only ran between Highgate and Crouch End.

During 1931 another 150 six-wheelers entered service, numbered LT 1052–1201. The first of these arrived in May 1931 and went to Dalston (D) garage for route 108D. Next, the T type at Nunhead was replaced by the larger LTs on route 621. In fact, the LT type displaced a number of the Ts which were then put to use on other services. Space does not permit a detailed description of the routes that received the new buses during the year but it is sufficient to say that by December 1931, when the last of the LTs was licensed, all the K types and larger Dennis buses had been replaced and withdrawn as had many of the S types. However, 24 of the sturdy S type saloons, already nine years old, were retained as spare vehicles and some lasted until 1936.

General built a trio of interesting saloons of its own in 1931. T1000–2 were designed and constructed at Chiswick and were powered by Meadows engines. Apart from their rather ungainly radiator and rounded cab they bore a certain similarity in appearance to the standard T types once the latter were rebuilt to front-entrance condition. T1000–2 were allocated to Kingston though they were often outstationed at Weybridge. In August and September 1932 the LGOC replaced the twelve Tilling-Stevens that Thomas Tilling operated on their behalf on route 109 with new Regals (T307–18). Tilling built the bodies which bore no resemblance to standard LGOC types, as 28-seaters, although their capacity was later increased to thirty.

On 16th September 1932 General inherited a batch of eleven non-standard single deckers when it took over the Royal Highlander and Loumax fleets.

In addition to the acquired vehicles, 319 single deck buses passed from General to the new London Passenger Transport Board on 1st July 1933. These consisted of 200 LT, 45 T, 24 S, one LS, four small Dennises and 42 Darts.

I would mention that this is by no means a complete history of London's single deck routes as it has not been possible to recall the many route variations or extensions that have taken place over the years, but is a story of the gradual development from the 16-seater solid-tyred bus of 1912 to the 35-seater six-wheeled vehicle of 1931. In conclusion, I would draw attention to revised route numbers which took effect from 3rd October 1934 when all single deck routes were numbered in the 200 series, and it may assist readers identifying the routes mentioned. The route numbers changed at that time were 41A to 232, 61 to 217, 62 to 218, 79 to 219, 87 to 234, 103 to 200, 104 to 240, 105 to 201, 108D to 208, 109 to 227, 110 to 210, 111 to 212, 113 to 213, 115 to 215, 137 to 237, 141 to 241, 154 to 233, 155B to 245, 171 to 214, 181B to 220, 187 to 247A, 195 to 228, 198 to 216, 263 to 236, 297 to 239, 305 to 246, 306 to 242, 353 to 221, 501 to 222, 505 to 223, 506 to 224, 538 to 238, 551 to 251, 603 to 244, 609 to 229, 621 to 243, G2 to 247, G3 to 248, G4 to 249, G5 to 252 and G7 to 250. Other routes numbered between 202 and 231 remained unchanged.

These were associated companies which had operated a number of services in west and north west London. Royal Highlander contributed nine out of the eleven. Six were normal control Duple-bodied Guy ONDs which became G1–6 in the LGOC numbering, and three were small Birch-bodied Beans with specially narrow bodies for operation on the Ealing–Greenford service (BN1–3). Loumax's fleet consisted of two United-bodied Guys (G7, 8) which, though only small vehicles, were unusual in being of the forward control ONDF type. A fourth Bean (BN4), also with Birch body, came earlier – in September 1930 – from Mrs Winifred Winter's Pinner Bus Service and had been of particular interest in that, though ostensibly owned by Mrs Winter, it had in fact been purchased and supplied to her by the LGOC as part of an operating arrangement between the two parties.

THE LAST OF THE LINE

Towards the end of the nineteen-twenties a short-lived craze developed for six wheeled double deck motor buses. It was spurred on by the pioneering activities of certain manufacturers, notably Guy and Karrier, who were endeavouring to maximise seating capacity, and was quickly taken up by many others. Six wheeled trolleybuses are, of course, a recent memory and a few diesel-powered vehicles have been built for special export markets in recent times, but at home the popularity of the six wheeled motor bus faded away as quickly as it had arisen. Comparatively few such vehicles were built after about 1933 and the last of all entered service in Leicester some forty years ago. Leicester's famous AEC Renowns are recalled briefly here.

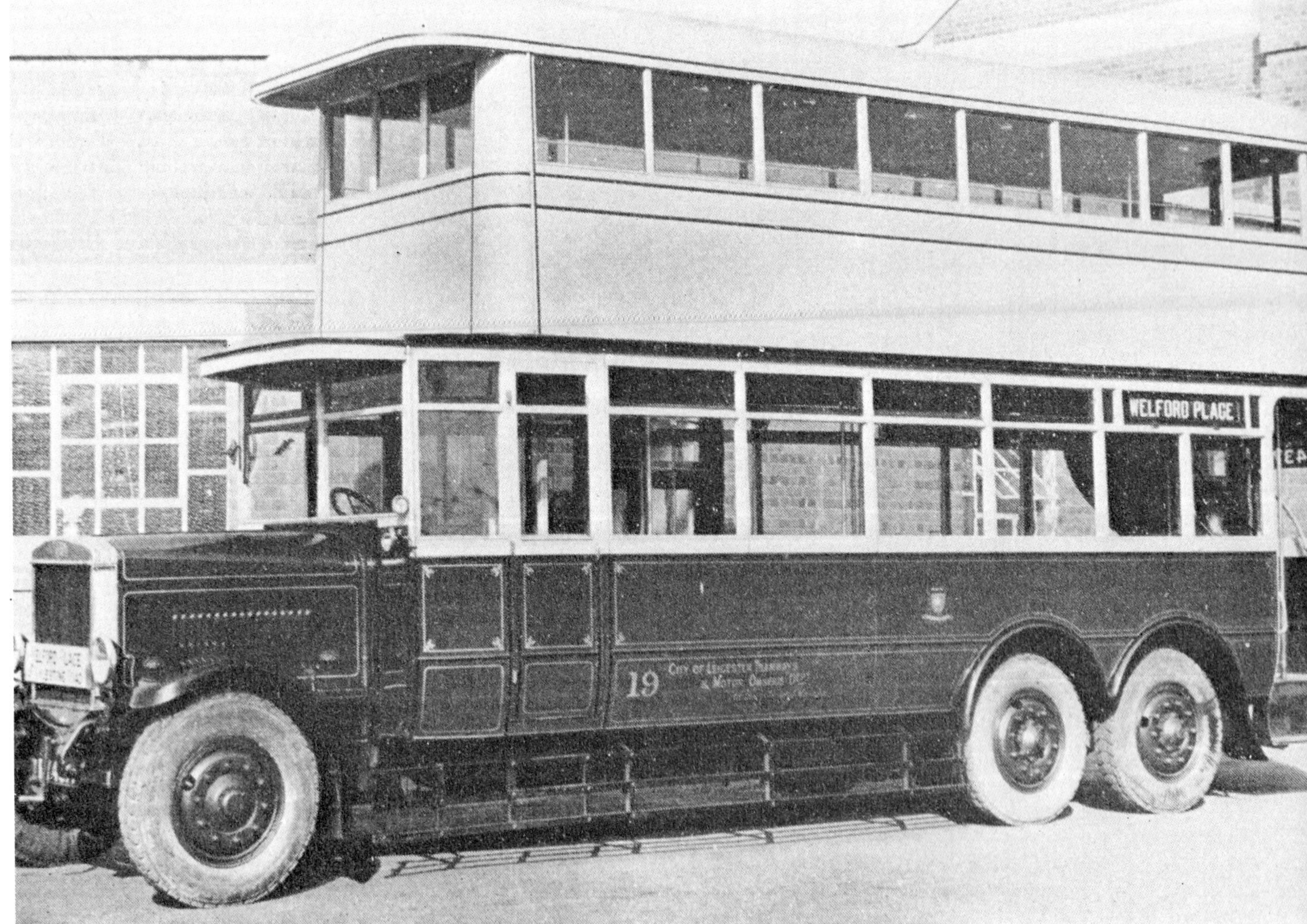

Leicester Corporation had been well to the fore in the purchase of six wheelers when these were all the rage, having acquired a fleet of 23 bonneted Guys between 1927 and 1929. All were Brush-bodied with enclosed staircases, and they were unusual in that their upper deck pillars did not match up with those on the lower deck. For its deliveries between 1931 and 1937 the Corporation turned to two axle vehicles, mostly Leyland Titans and AEC Regents, but in 1939 six wheelers came on the scene once again. The Corporation had decided upon a tram scrapping programme and its general manager, the well remembered Ben England, specified the largest possible buses in order to achieve a seating capacity in line with that of the trams which were being replaced. Nine AEC Regents were ordered with Northern Counties bodies seating 64–32 on each deck. They entered service on the first major stage of the programme, the conversion of the King Edward's Road route on 3rd April 1939, and were given numbers 321–329 in the Corporation's fleet (CBC 913–921).

The bodies were a stretched version of Northern Counties' standard product which at the time was the most distinctive on the market with its very rounded front dome and thick corner pillars, and its bulbous driving cab. As always, Northern Counties provided a robust jig-built body using solid section cold-drawn steel frames. The lower saloon was very well appointed, especially in having deep chromium plated surrounds to the windows and a pale blue enamelled ceiling, but the upper deck [as seen in the photograph] was rather spartan in being single skinned with all the hoops of the roof showing. An old fashioned feature was the fitting of pneumatically worked bells, reminiscent of tramway practice, but these were replaced by normal electric ones in later life.

The second and last batch of Renowns was built in 1940. There were 16 of them [330–345, DBC 221–236], bringing the Leicester six-wheel total to 25. Though they resembled the earlier batch fairly closely, the bodies were actually built at Washwood Heath by Metro Cammell. The Northern Counties front and rear dome styling was fairly faithfully copied as were the striking curves of the lower saloon end windows. They were distinguishable by a flatter cab and by the addition of a handsome multi-row bumper at the rear, and the standard maroon and cream livery was brightened by the use of orange lining on the moulding separating the two. Six of the Metro Cammell Renowns are seen when new outside the Abbey Park Road depot.

The 25 Renowns served Leicester very well for many years, the last ones finally bidding farewell to the City on the evening of 30th June 1958. They survived all other six wheeled double deck motor buses by several years and became a great favourite with enthusiasts in their later years. They were popular, too, with their drivers which was perhaps surprising as they were powered only by 7.7 engines which, in theory, were rather small for the size of the vehicles. However, they coped successfully with heavy loads, helped no doubt by Leicester's fairly flat terrain. They had Wilson preselector gearboxes and fluid flywheel transmission. The last one to be built, Metro Cammell-bodied no 345, is seen (right-hand photo, second row) outside the Humberstone Gate depot waiting to start out on an early enthusiasts' tour of the Leicester system in September 1952.

The last of the Northern Counties batch to operate in passenger service was no 329, withdrawn in May 1958 after completing 651,856 miles. Shortly afterwards it was presented by the Corporation for preservation to the Vintage Passenger Vehicle Society, one of the component bodies that went to form the now-powerful Historic Commercial Vehicle Club. The only condition attached to the gift was that the bus should remain in Leicester livery. It is seen here on an enthusiasts' outing in April 1959 at the Leighton Buzzard yard of Buckmaster Coaches in company with another very interesting double decker, the second Leyland Atlantean prototype, XTC 684. Nowadays the bus is back in its home town undergoing lengthy restoration.

THE SOUTH WALES HILL BUSES

**Fifty years ago and more the provision of regular bus services over routes
containing very steep gradients presented a great problem.
Such were the frailties and shortage of pulling power of most buses then available
that they simply could not cope with this type of work. CHRIS TAYLOR recalls
how two South Wales operators turned to a Swiss vehicle manufacturer
to solve their problem and looks at the later generations of special buses
that also operated on two of the country's most notorious routes.**

ON high, overlooking Swansea from an altitude of some 570 ft is the Townhill estate. Towards the end of the last century, when the city's upper reaches were still largely undeveloped, the area was served by a 0.19-mile-long cable tramway owned by the Swansea Constitution Hill Incline Tramway Co Ltd. It opened in 1898 but quickly proved to be a financial disaster and enjoyed only a brief three-year existence, being closed down in 1901. Townhill remained unserved by public transport for many years thereafter and residents had no option but to make the tiring climb on foot.

The lack of adequate transport to the Townhill area from central Swansea was a problem which became increasingly acute from 1909 onwards as the dwellers from slum clearance areas in other parts of the city were rehoused by the council on a steadily expanding new estate. An electric tramway was promoted in 1913 but the coming of World War I put paid to the venture and the problem remained unsolved.

Once the war was over the estate resumed its growth on an increasing scale and the transport problem grew along with it in an ever-worsening degree. By now the need for a bus ser-

vice from Townhill into Swansea was thoroughly recognised but the problem was that suitably powerful vehicles were not available. Though only 1½ miles long, the route involved an average gradient of 1 in 9.6 with the steepest section at 1 in 5.6, and this meant too taxing a schedule for the vehicles then on the market. It was not until December 1925 that a solution was found. The Swiss manufacturer, Saurer, demonstrated one of its 3AD chassis to representatives of the South Wales Transport Company and the Swansea Council's Watch and Tramways Committees, and it was a

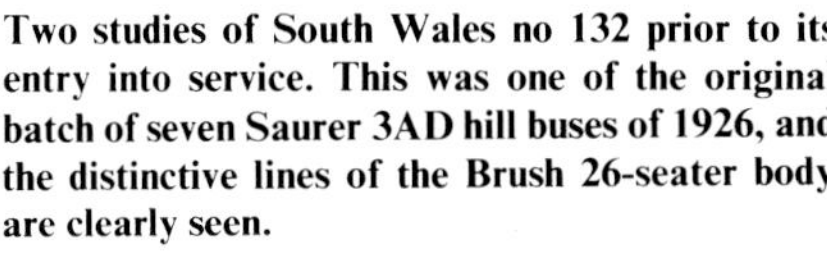

Two studies of South Wales no 132 prior to its entry into service. This was one of the original batch of seven Saurer 3AD hill buses of 1926, and the distinctive lines of the Brush 26-seater body are clearly seen.

No longer in pristine condition, the same Saurer is seen near the end of its life showing signs of the hard work encountered on the Townhill run. The Saurers had very prominent front wheel hub covers and a distinctive curved radiator guard.

The prototype AEC Renown was demonstrated in 1933 and carried full South Wales livery though still owned at this stage by the chassis manufacturer. A notice in the front bulkhead window leaves travellers in no doubt as to the true ownership of the vehicle. At the time it was by far the largest vehicle ever to have operated on the Townhill route.

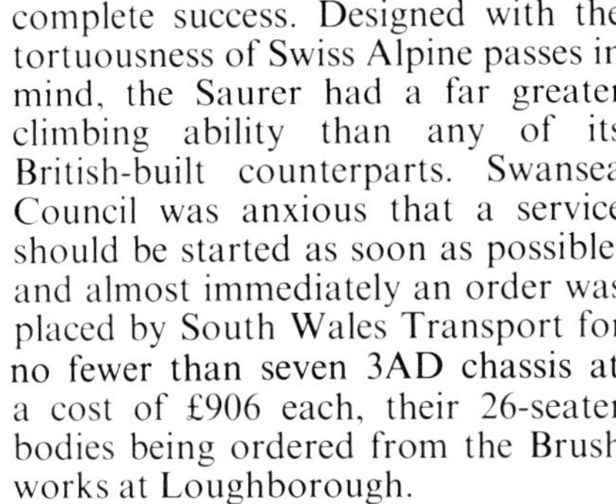

complete success. Designed with the tortuousness of Swiss Alpine passes in mind, the Saurer had a far greater climbing ability than any of its British-built counterparts. Swansea Council was anxious that a service should be started as soon as possible, and almost immediately an order was placed by South Wales Transport for no fewer than seven 3AD chassis at a cost of £906 each, their 26-seater bodies being ordered from the Brush works at Loughborough.

The seven Saurers were built very quickly and were delivered during April and May 1926 as South Wales nos 129–35 (CY 8676–82). Sufficient were in stock for the service to commence on 22nd April. To forestall any fears over safety, each was fitted with a variable camshaft so that the engine acted as a brake on the downward journey, and there was a sprag and a second speed lock on the gearbox. The residents of Townhill had to be persuaded of the safety of the new buses, and to prove the point many free rides were given at the inauguration of the service. Drivers were also specially trained, a practice which continued for many years such was the arduous nature of the service. When in use on the Townhill service, the Saurers never had a chance to get into a higher gear than second, and as a result, fuel consumption was astronomical at 3.1mpg. Even when in use on other services when not required on the Townhill run they proved thirsty machines and had to be refuelled after a few journeys.

The new service was an immediate success and further vehicles became necessary. Two more Brush-bodied 26-seaters arrived on the scene in December 1926 (148–9 CY 9451–2) whilst four 32-seaters with bodies built by the operator were placed into service between March and July 1928 (175–8 WN 862–5). The Saurer continued to be the only suitable chassis and further expansion in June and July 1930 led to the arrival of four more machines, this time with SWT 28-seat bodywork

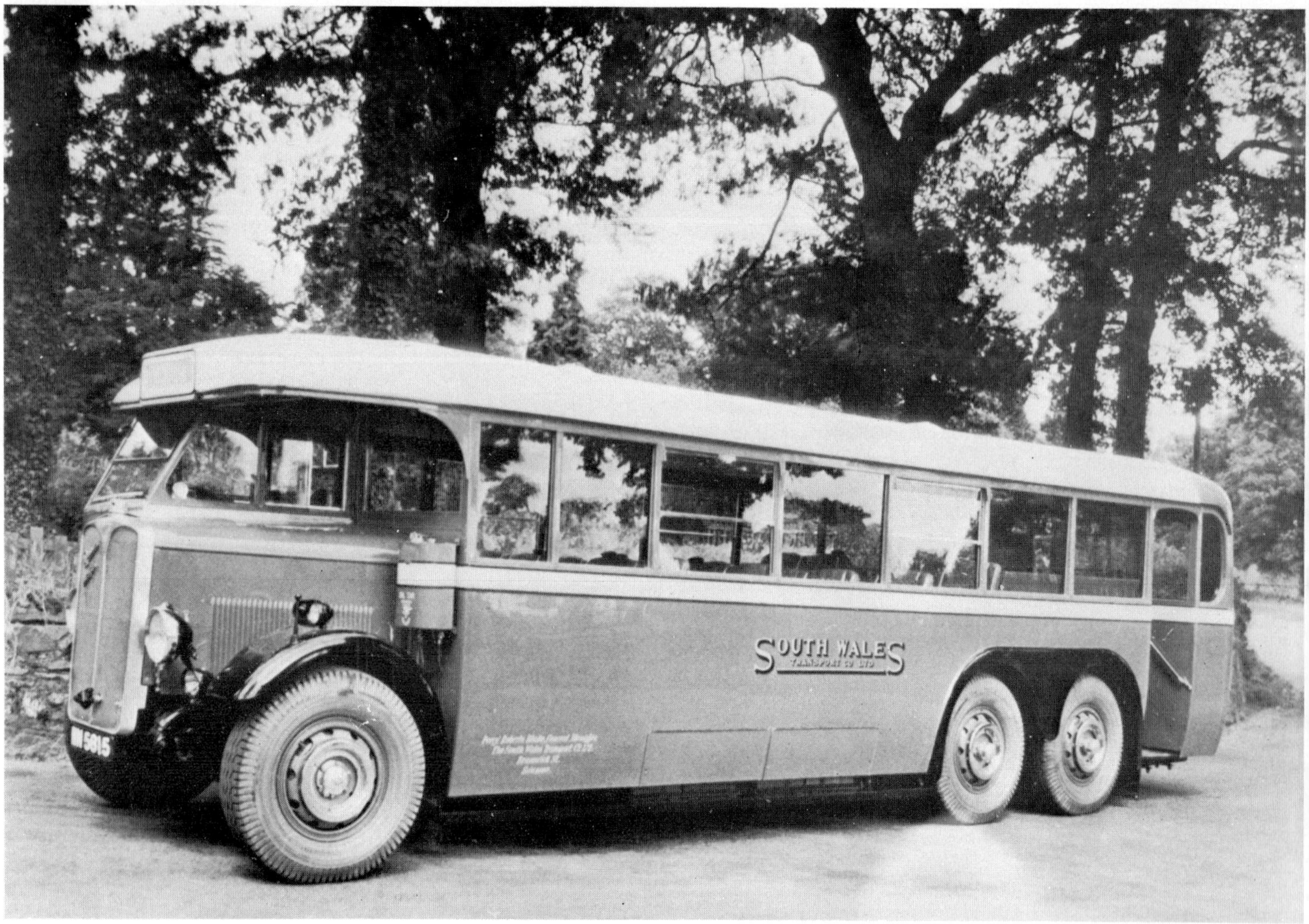
SOUTH WALES
TRANSPORT CO LTD

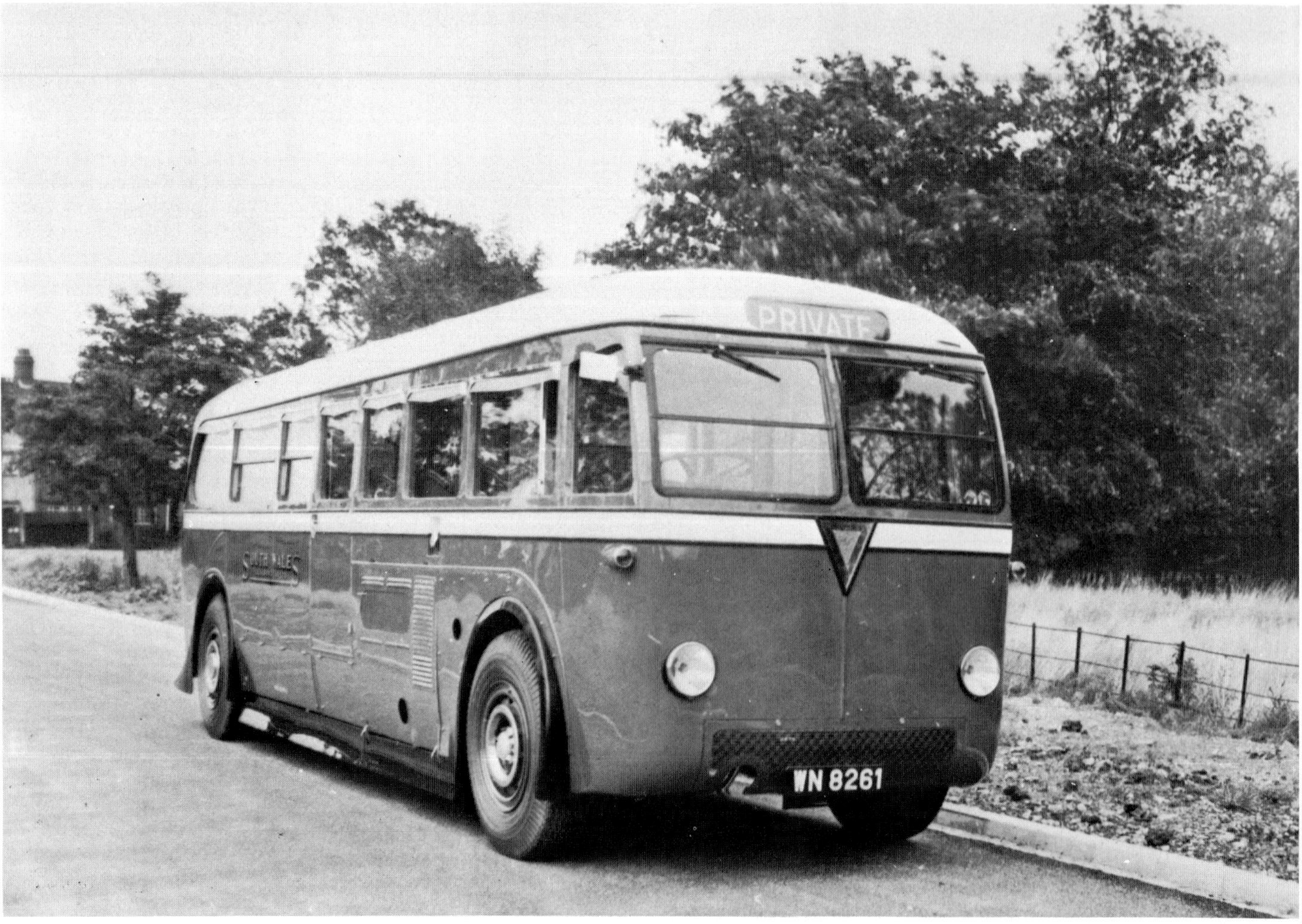
PRIVATE
SOUTH WALES
WN 8261

The last of the five Renowns purchased by South Wales in 1933 as Saurer replacements. The Brush body has a rear entrance as against the front entrance layout on the Park Royal-bodied demonstrator. Though built to a high specification these vehicles did not come up to expectations.

In theory the AEC Q was hardly a suitable choice for continuous operation on steep hills, and South Wales certainly had trouble with them on the Townhill route. No 361 was one of five Brush-bodied 40-seaters purchased in the summer of 1933.

By the late nineteen-thirties special buses were no longer considered necessary for the Townhill gradient. A 1939 purchase was this Brush-bodied 39-seater, one of a batch of very late Renowns with fully-floating rear axles which saw general use throughout South Wales' operating territory.

(227–30 WN 3099–3102). A stock of seventeen Saurers had now been built up, which was undoubtedly the largest bus fleet of this make in the country. They worked hard, the service ultimately building up to a 5 minute schedule on five days of the week, augmented to a bus every 2½ minutes at the busiest periods on Saturdays. This gave 223 trips up the hill on Mondays to Thursdays, 238 on Fridays and 288 on Saturdays, a total of 1418 per week. People living along the bus route obviously did not get much peace except on Sundays when the service took its day of rest.

By 1933 the original vehicles were nearing the end of their lives, and with the cost of fuel rising, SWT was spurred on to find a more economical replacement. Experiments commenced with an AEC Renown six-wheeler fitted with 8.8 litre diesel engine, preselective gearbox coupled to a fluid flywheel, vacuum hydraulic brakes with sprag attachment and a Park Royal 38-seater body. MV 371, which was a thoroughly modern vehicle, had started life as an AEC-owned demonstrator in October 1932, but it was purchased by SWT in June 1933 and given fleet number 316. It had proved sufficiently satisfactory to encourage the purchase of five more vehicles which had already been allocated fleet numbers 311–15 (WN 5811–15). They arrived on the scene in August 1933 and were put into service almost immediately. Unlike the demonstrator, they were equipped with Brush bodies and had the slightly increased seating capacity of forty.

The cost of the Renowns, at £1770 each, was high and, sad to say, they did not perform as well on the Townhill run as the performance of the demonstrator had led the company to hope. There was continued trouble with them, which included warped and cracked cylinder heads, bearing failures and collapsed differentials, the last-named requiring a complete re-design by AEC of the rear axle assembly. Fuel consumption at 5.73mpg was a big improvement over the Saurers but was lower than had been expected.

Further Saurer replacements were needed, but because of the troubles with the Renowns it was decided not to purchase any more. Instead, experiments took place in 1934 with a Daimler COG5 and an AEC Q type oiler. As was only to be expected in view of its small capacity engine, the Daimler proved very slow but fuel consumption was excellent at 7.46mpg. To overcome the slowness, various rear axle ratios were tried and this must have proved a success as five were ordered to replace Saurers. The AEC Q gave some engine trouble and returned a fuel consumption of 5.98mpg, which was only a little better than that of the Renowns and, in typical Q type fashion, it used large quantities of lubricating oil.

The five Daimlers entered service in February and March 1935 (338–42 WN 7738–42) and they were fitted with Weymann bodies seating thirty-five. They had 5-speed gearboxes and 7:1 rear axle ratios, and proved an immediate success in returning a creditable 8.41mpg. They were bargains at £1550 each but, strangely, they were not re-specified for the final clear-out of the Saurers later in 1935. South Wales Transport was a BET-group subsidiary and – with notable exceptions such as Trent – these were not Daimler fans. South Wales itself was firmly wedded

The first Bargoed Hill Saurer as originally built for Lewis & James of Newbridge. The rather old fashioned though solidly built Dodson body seated thirty.

Taken from a Saurer advert is this photo of the second West Mon Saurer descending a steep part of Bargoed Hill. It shows the original 27-seater rear entrance body that fell apart after only three years' service.

The original West Mon Leyland Bull, with Dodson 32-seater dual-door body, is seen climbing up from beneath the Brecon & Merthyr Railway bridge to Aberbargoed on its way to Markham.

to AEC, Leyland and Dennis. The comparatively low seating capacity of the COG5s may have also told against them.

Despite the less than satisfactory performance of the AEC Q demonstrator on the Townhill run, five such vehicles were ordered from Southall, complete with 39-seat Brush bodies (360–4 WN 8260–4) and they cost £1650 apiece. Delivery was spread over five months between June and October 1935, and whilst this was going on SWT purchased the Weymann-bodied demonstrator (BML 488) and numbered it 365. Once again the problem of very high lubricating oil consumption was quickly encountered, and it was one which the manufacturer seemed unable to eradicate. Main bearing failures were another major problem and lead-bronze bearings had to be substituted along with increased bore oil pipes to keep them adequately lubricated. A further modification was the provision of special sumps fitted with a small basin so that the bearings were not uncovered on the hill.

A total of 34 vehicles was specially bought for the Townhill service over a period of 9½ years. As can be seen, the only really successful ones in terms of combining good performance, reliability and economy were the five Daimler COG5s. Such were the advances in design that no further special vehicles were thought necessary for the Townhill run which nowadays is maintained by nothing more exotic than Leyland Nationals.

Eastwards from Swansea, on the border between Glamorgan and Monmouthshire (now Gwent), is the town of Bargoed lying in the Rhymney river valley. Back in the mid-twenties the firm of Lewis & James of Newbridge was a sizeable operator who wished to operate a service from Bargoed to Markham in the Sirhowy Valley to connect with other services and to save a roundabout journey. There was a problem in that the direct road from Bargoed to Markham via Aberbargoed included some difficult gradients for part of the journey. The steepest was a 250ft stretch of 1 in 4½ but there was also 500ft of 1 in 5 and 1220ft of

The third of the pre-war Leylands carried a Weymann body, the modern appearance of which was marred by the outdated style of radiator which was by this time no longer in use on the builder's passenger vehicle range. Because of its super-overdrive gearbox, no 13 was often used on the long distance Cardiff-Markham service.

The same vehicle is seen after its original Weymann body had been replaced by a Burlingham wartime style body. The photo shows how difficult it was for drivers to judge when to turn on driving out from beneath the railway bridge.

1 in 8, including an awkward right-angled bend under a low bridge at the foot of the hill.

Lewis & James had no doubt heard about SWT's negotiation with Saurer and early in 1926 they approached the manufacturer to build a special chassis for the Bargoed-Markham route. A demonstration run was carried out about April and this resulted in an order for a single 3AD model. Christopher Dodson was given the contract for a 30-seater body and the complete vehicle, with wheel ratchet sprags and similar engine braking as on the SWT Saurers, cost £1750. It was

The first Foden, no 1, is seen leaving a trail of exhaust smoke as it descends the hill. It carries the original body transferred from the Leyland Bull of 1930, delivery delays having made it preferable to re-use the old body rather than to wait for a new one to be constructed.

A rear view of the same Foden shows its ancestry as it dives beneath the railway bridge. Note the semi-cross country type tyres fitted at the rear.

delivered in September 1926 carrying Lewis & James' lavender blue livery and Western & Sirhowy Valley's fleet name, and was tried out first of all in Hill Street, Newport, before a party of local officials.

A couple of problems lay in the way of the operation of the Saurer. First of all, there was a question mark over the future of some of the Lewis & James operations. The West Monmouthshire Omnibus Board was in the process of being formed, its Bill in Parliament having received Royal Assent on 4th August 1926. Agreement had been made between Lewis & James and the Board that, if licences were obtained, the Board would take over the Hill route together with five other services within its area. And there was the attitude of Gelligaer UDC to be taken into account. Bargoed lay within the UDC's boundaries and the council was not willing to give a licence for the service to operate. The bus appears to have remained idle until it was sold to the West Monmouthshire Omnibus Board in February 1927 for £1500. It finally entered service on the Bargoed–Markham run after a number of inspections of its intended route by council officials and inspectors from the Ministry of Transport, but before this it was used on other services licensed to the Board. Permission was finally given for the service to start in June 1927, originally for an experimental period of a month.

The service was an overnight success, receipts very quickly reaching a staggering 13.33d per mile. The need for an additional vehicle was immediately recognised and a second Saurer was ordered. It was basically similar to its predecessor except that, at the Ministry of Transport's insistence, the hub caps were modified to project only 3½ins from the wheels as against 4ins on the standard design. The Saurer chassis cost £1109, making it a very expensive proposition bearing in mind that a Leyland Lion could be purchased, complete with body, for £1240. Money was very tight with the Board as all the cash required to purchase buses from the companies taken over had been borrowed, so a body had to be found for the new chassis that was as cheap as possible. A 27-seater was ordered from United of Lowestoft for £400 and the new vehicle (fleet no 9, WO 974) duly arrived in October 1927, allowing a better service to be given. Its predecessor, AX 9617, had meanwhile been numbered 13, a number which subsequently became famous by being used for successive 'Hill' buses.

Vintage transport in 1956. The last remaining example of the Bargoed Hill Leylands waits at the Bargoed terminus and looks ancient though still sounding very healthy. The chassis is now privately preserved though the Burlingham body, unfortunately, no longer exists.

The second West Mon Foden was delivered in June 1952 and carried 35-seater bodywork by Willowbrook of Loughborough. The first Foden received an almost identical body a year later.

Obviously people in the area were less superstitious than those in other parts of the country where the fleet number 13 was studiously avoided.

Thoughts were given to purchasing a third Saurer but it was not until 1929, when the bearings on the original one were in a state of collapse, that anything positive was done. Saurer were again approached, but hedging their bets, the management also had talks with another manufacturer, whose identity was not revealed at the time. In December 1929 a Thornycroft six-wheeler loaded to 3 tons was tried out on the hill; its performance was described as good but a 5-ton load was required and it could not cope with this. Saurer were the next visitors in February 1930, but again the load-carrying capacity was not good enough. Meanwhile, Leyland were waiting on the sidelines and stated that they were willing to construct a suitable bus, probably as much for the publicity value as for any other reason. They employed their Bull goods chassis, one of which was fitted with a Dodson 32-seat dual-entrance body. The vehicle was complete by September 1930 and after being tested on other hills around Blackwood it was finally tried out on Bargoed Hill with the equivalent of 53 seated and 10 standing passengers, and it passed with flying colours. The chassis was altered from standard in having sprag gear to prevent running backwards, and the handbrake applied to all four wheels, it being arranged to act as the actual service brake. The servo mechanism activated the rear wheel brakes.

The Leyland took fleet number 1 (WO 4625) and it was an immediate success, although it was the victim of a slight accident in Bargoed in October 1930 when the conductor let off the handbrake. Its arrival allowed the temporary withdrawal of the newer of the two Saurers which went away for a new body to be fitted, the original one having rotted very badly, proving that it is not always wise to buy the cheapest. So successful was the Bull that two further Leylands followed in December 1931 (10 WO 5913) and July 1935 (13 AAX 27) respectively. No 10 was again one of Leyland's Bull models although of the more modern TQ3 type as against the earlier TQ1 type of no 1. No 13, though very similar in appearance to its predecessors, was officially a Leyland Alpine Beaver chassis of type TSC9 and it was modified in similar fashion to the Bulls, plus the addition of an overdrive gearbox

to make it more suitable for normal service when not required on the Bargoed Hill run. No 10 was Dodson-bodied, but this manufacturer had gone out of business before the second no 13 came on the scene, and the body contract for this one went to Weymann. It carried 32 as against 30 on the dual-entrance Bulls. Both the Saurers were duly withdrawn, no 13 in 1936 and no 9 in 1939, although the newer one stayed in the fleet as a towing wagon right through to 1946. It was the only vehicle capable of towing a disabled bus off Bargoed Hill.

The Leylands gave excellent service on the Hill route. The third one had been delivered with an oil engine, the other two having been converted to this form of propulsion in October and November 1934. Their lives were uneventful until the end of the war when nos 10 and 13 received new semi-utility bodies by Burlingham. Replacement did not commence until 1949 when the only manufacturer willing to supply special vehicles was Foden, who supplied a PVSC6 chassis in July 1949. Registered HWO 590, it received its predecessor's fleet no 1 and it also inherited the Dodson body from the former no 1. This body, which had

been extensively rebuilt by Meredith of Blackwood and was now a 31-seater with rear entrance, having lost its front entrance in the process, still retained its original outline and looked incongruously old fashioned when mounted on the modern Foden chassis.

A second new Foden followed in June 1952 (30 KWO 368) but in this case a very handsome new Willowbrook 31-seat body was fitted, and a year later the first Foden received a similar body. The last Bull continued in service until 1959 when quotations were received from three manufacturers for a chassis to be fitted with a

Willowbrook body:

AEC	£2726
Foden	£2928
Leyland	£2526

All were specified as including sprag gear and, not surprisingly, a Leyland was purchased. The third no 13 (UWO 688) arrived in March 1959 with a great deal of publicity. It was 7ft 6ins wide and was based on a modified Leyland Titan double deck chassis. Its life on the Bargoed Hill route was not very long as, at the end of 1962, the hill was bypassed by a new route via a recently built housing estate. The Leyland was rebodied in July 1966 by Massey as a conventional double decker, the two Fodens being withdrawn in 1965 after a spell on normal service.

Today the hill is hardly recognisable as the right-angled bend under the railway is no more, the railway having been lifted, and the road has been widened and the bridge demolished. Ordinary coaches now climb the hill with a bit of an effort though some still get caught out on the gradient. The author worked on one of the last buses on the route and can vouch for the great excitement that the trip gave. It is a great loss that it has gone.

Last of the line. The final hill bus, a Leyland PD2/38, delivered in 1959, carried a Willowbrook 31-seater body of very outdated style; it was probably the last new half-cab single decker ever built. Note that the road surface is a lot better than in earlier photos.

NORTHERN ENTERPRISE

**Spasmodically over the years a prominent bus operator,
the Northern General Transport Company, has produced
some very interesting buses of its own. Such enterprise is not always rewarded,
but in this case it was and Northern generally got good service
from the vehicles it designed. KEN BLACKER outlines the interesting vehicles,
new and rebuilt, that emerged from the Bensham works.**

THROUGHOUT its long and complex history the British bus industry has thrown up surprisingly few cases of operators who have ventured into the realms of designing and building their own vehicles. Traditionally this work has been left in the hands of specialist manufacturers who, though normally proving equal to the task, have sometimes failed to provide the types of vehicle required to meet specific needs or whose products have fallen short in terms of performance and reliability. Even in quite recent times the inability of manufacturers to keep in step with operators' needs has resulted in severe problems for both sides of the industry as those who have had dealings with some of the unhappy rear-engined models of the later nineteen-sixties or early seventies will readily confirm.

One of the rare pioneering companies which, in days gone by, was ambitious enough to produce its own buses was the Northern General Transport Co Ltd. As in most instances of outstanding enterprise

there was a dominant personality working behind the scenes, and in the case of Northern it was Major (later Colonel) Gordon W Hayter, who joined the company in 1922 as its chief engineer, becoming also its general manager fourteen years later. Though short in stature, he was a forceful personality. A trained engineer and pioneer motorist, Major Hayter had begun his apprenticeship in 1903 with the Motor Manufacturing Company and later worked for Daimler and Humber. He enlisted in the ASC motor transport section at the outbreak of war in 1914 and subsequently served in France and Italy where he was mentioned in dispatches; he later recorded a piece of military history by writing a book on the work of the Motor Transport Section with the Italian Expeditionary Forces. When he joined Northern the company was still less than ten years old. It had begun operations in November 1913 by putting eight single deckers to work on a six mile service from Low Fell to Chester-le-Street, and by the time the Great War came along to stifle expansion the fleet had grown to fifty-four. Post-war development was rapid, and in 1921 the company opened its central engineering depot and administrative headquarters at Queen Street, Bensham, Gateshead. 1922 saw the opening of Sunderland, Murton and Consett depots

and by 1927 a fleet of 266 vehicles was actively engaged on a network of 37 services which still form the core of the company's activities today.

Right from the time it opened the Bensham works, Northern was engaged on heavy reconstruction of vehicles in addition to the normal overhaul processes. The company standardised on Daimlers in the early post-war years and had about 114 vehicles of the make in service by 1924. Six were Y type coaches and a further half-dozen were 29-seat pneumatic-tyred saloons, but the great majority were models bought at knock-down prices from the War Department's surplus stock and rebuilt by the company ready for the fitting of bus bodies. Many were originally short wheelbase chassis, and their conversion involved major reconstruction as most were extended to a wheelbase of 16ft which involved the fitting of new chassis side-members, transmission etc. When equipped with a saloon body they were, to all intents and purposes, new vehicles, and many of these major rebuilds were given Northern's own chassis numbers in a series starting from one upwards. The only non-Daimlers in the fleet in the early post-war years were six little ex-Flying Corps Crossley tenders and these had also been extensively rebuilt before being transformed into 14-seat

Bygone days in Chester-le-Street. Photographed in January 1924, long before the little town was inundated with traffic hurtling along the main Newcastle-Durham road, are three Northerns and an independent leisurely awaiting their respective times of departure. All are Daimlers, and the three Northern ones are typical of the many that the company extensively rebuilt in the early nineteen-twenties.

buses.

In 1924 Northern began purchasing vehicles manufactured by a fellow BET subsidiary, Midland Red, whose SOS chassis were operationally very satisfactory, having been designed and built by an operator for an operator. For its massive expansion programme of the late nineteen-twenties Northern standardised on SOS's of various models, both new and secondhand, although AECs also came on the scene from 1932 onwards. However, by this time Major Hayter and the engineering department staff at Bensham were well advanced in designing a bus of their own.

Northern had a problem in that its area was over-endowed with low railway bridges which prevented the use of double deckers on a large scale. Even as late as 1933 there were only 14 such vehicles in the entire fleet (13 AEC and 1 SOS). However, some very heavy passenger traffic was en-

countered on many services and the company was anxious to obtain single deckers with a seating capacity considerably in excess of the normal figure of about thirty-four. A seated load of 45 was considered desirable to deal with colliery and factory peaks and with the heavy movements on trunk routes, notably the summer traffic on the Newcastle–South Shields run. There was nothing on the market at the time with a capacity anywhere near approaching this figure, so the company had no option but to design its own. Major Hayter and his team had obviously been impressed by AEC's Q type which, by placing the engine vertically on the offside, released space at the front and increased carrying capacity. But at the time the Q had only been produced in two-axle form which, under the restrictions then in force, limited its overall length and kept the capacity down below forty. Northern needed to go to the full permissible length of 30ft and thus required a third axle, and they also wanted to eliminate a notable shortcoming in the AEC design. This was the untidy internal layout caused by the projection of the engine into the passenger saloon, necessitating the use of an inward-facing seat which was space wasting. They set about designing a chassis based generally on the Q type but with a double rear bogie and with a more compact engine design which did not project into the passenger area. Their SE6 (Side-Engined 6-wheeler) of 1933 was the outcome.

Northern's no 586 (CN 5674) was an impressive machine both in design and appearance. It employed a narrow chassis frame supplied by Rubery Owen on which the side members were equidistant throughout their length and level apart from a slight arch over the rear axles. The narrowness of the frame enabled the engine to be located comfortably on the offside, and it also gave room for the differential to be mounted outside the frame between the offside spring and the side member, resulting in a completely straight drive line between the two. The springs were attached to outriggers on the chassis and there was a novel rear suspension arrangement which resulted in each axle having two springs with a balance beam between the front and rear springs of the bogie, excessive movement of which was prevented by an auxiliary damper-spring arrangement. Only the forward axle was driven, the company claiming that it had found by experiment that a rear bogie driven on all four wheels did not perform as well as its own two-wheel-drive design. Sir W G Armstrong

Whitworth & Co built the rear axle assembly on Tyneside to Northern's specifications.

One of Northern's biggest problems lay in finding a power unit sufficiently compact to lie vertically outside the chassis frame without protruding significantly into the passenger saloon. They scoured the home market but found nothing suitable and ended up by taking the unusual step of importing an engine from the USA. This was a Hercules WXRT 6-cylinder petrol unit of 6.3 litres with bore and stroke of 4ins and 4½ins respectively and it was largely on account of its comparatively short stroke and the side valve layout that an engine of unusually compact design was attainable. The Hercules engine had a good reputation for reliability, being the offside one of a pair of power units used on the novel American Twin Coach design, and thus had the advantage that the valve gear and accessories were on the correct side. Power was transmitted from the engine through an unusual, hydraulically-operated Borg & Beck clutch to a four-speed Fuller gearbox, which was also of American manufacture. Braking was a combination of Marelli vacuum servo and Lockheed hydraulic power transmission for the footbrake which operated on all six wheels, the hand brake being linked only to the rear drums. Unlike AEC on its Q type, Northern considered a front-mounted radiator necessary, a set of comparatively long pipes being required to

link it to the engine, and another variation from the AEC Q was in the position of the front axle which was placed well forward, giving a rather long wheelbase. The petrol tank and batteries were mounted outside the frame on the nearside and their weight balanced to a large extent that of the engine and transmission units.

No 586 was given chassis number 64, which presumably followed on from the last of the earlier Daimler rebuilds. It went to Rochester for the fitting by Short Bros of its 45-seater body on which all seats but one faced forwards. The main entrance was just behind the front axle and there was a double seat forward of it alongside the driver from which a very good view could be had of the road ahead. The vehicle had a very low roof line which was achieved partly by employing a sunken gangway about 6ins lower than the seating areas, and by the omission of internal luggage racks. As with many Northern service bus designs over the years, the interior of the body was rather spartan, even to a single-skinned roof, although the leather and moquette-covered seats were deeper than usual and gave a good standard of comfort.

The new bus was the star of a private viewing in London on 25th July, after which it entered service on the Newcastle–South Shields run where it performed encouragingly well. The Hercules engine was particularly smooth and quiet in

A brand new look for 1933. The prototype SE6 was impressive in appearance and looked even longer than its 30ft thanks to its low roof line. It was rather trolleybus-like at the front despite the presence of the large, low-mounted radiator grille, and in this view the side panel has been removed to show the particularly neat and compact setting of the Hercules engine.

The prototype SE6 from the nearside showing the entry behind the front axle that was to be moved forwards on production versions. This view shows it on delivery and proudly proclaiming its Short Bros. bodywork.

operation. By the end of 1935 no. 586 had covered more than 180,000 miles without any undue problems, but by this time it had been joined by two batches of production model SE6s. The first batch was a small one of five vehicles (604-8 CN 6100-4) upon which construction had commenced in the latter part of 1933 and which entered service between January and August 1934. Like the prototype, they had Short Bros bodies and in many respects they were very similar. However, they were most noticeably different in that the front axle was now set back, as on the Q type, permitting an entrance ahead of it adjacent to the driver in the manner that we nowadays accept as normal. There was no door at the entrance itself, but a sliding door in the front bulkhead separated the passenger saloon from the entrance area. The frontal design was very neat, there being only two fairly shallow steps from ground level to the gangway. Internally, the seating capacity was reduced by one to 44, all facing forwards, and there was a slight hump in the floor over the engine compartment. Sloping pillars and a downward sweep at the rear of the lower waistrail moulding gave a much more sleek and modern appearance than on 586.

Encouraged by the continuing good performance of its home-produced fleet, Northern embarked on a more ambitious construction programme for 1935, embrac-

ing no fewer than 31 SE6s. Six of these (651-6 CN 6610-15) were to be 28-seat touring coaches, twenty more were to be normal 45-seat buses (657-76 CN 6616-35) whilst the remaining five, though also service buses, were earmarked for the subsidiary Tynemouth & District fleet in which they were allocated fleet numbers 82-6 (FT 3478-82). The five buses of 1934 carried chassis numbers 65-9 and the batch of 31 followed on from this, chassis 70-94 being allocated to the saloons (though not in numerical order) and 95-100 to the coaches, again out of sequence. Unlike their predecessors, the 1935 batch were not built at Bensham, the works being too fully occupied to undertake a construction programme of this magnitude at the time. Instead the work was subcontracted to AEC who assembled the chassis at Southall. Though basically similar to the 604-8 batch, they differed in employing a four-speed David Brown gearbox in place of the Fuller unit, and they also had David Brown rear axle gearing. All but one of the saloons had Short Bros composite bodies similar to the earlier batch, but no 676, which did not eventually enter service until 1936, received a Weymann metal framed body which was very similar in appearance to the others.

The six coaches were something really special. Also bodied by Short, they had only 28 seats in a most luxurious two and one arrangement. They were intended for

the company's growing programme of extended tours and came on the road in time for the peak of the 1935 season. Prior to their arrival the SE6 had only been seen operating around Tyneside and in parts of County Durham; now specimens were to be seen as far afield as the Scottish Highlands, Snowdonia and the Cornish Riviera. In order to obtain maximum performance the coaches had a slightly larger Hercules WXLC3 engine with $4\frac{1}{4}$ins bore $\times 4\frac{3}{4}$ins stroke and capacity of 6.65 litres. The higher capacity was useful to cope with a body weight some $\frac{3}{4}$ ton heavier than that of the saloons. As built, the coaches had a fully opening, canvas-covered roof over the centre section of the body, but just before the war this was replaced by a more solid arrangement with fixed glass cant panels and a sliding centre section. The SE6 coaches had better manoeuvrability than many smaller vehicles, climbed well on hills and with their exceptionally quiet running engines they made really excellent touring vehicles. If there was a complaint that could be levelled against them it was that luggage space sometimes bordered on the inadequate, especially as there were no inside luggage racks, but this problem was overcome during their late thirties rebuilding when a large roof rack was provided. At the same time their unladen weight rose yet again to 7 tons 4 cwt.

Though Northern had earlier proclaimed itself satisfied with the adhesion of the six-wheelers with their single driving axle, the performance was, in truth, sometimes less than satisfactory. The company's operating terrain was prone to becoming ice or snow covered during winter months, and there were often occasions when insufficient grip could be obtained on the SE6 because of adhesion difficulties where the load was spread over two axles of which only one drove. Besides, the complicated rear bogie and springing arrangement led to maintenance problems. It was decided to build a two axle variant on the basic design as part of Bensham's 1936 construction programme, to which was allocated the chassis no 101. Fleet number 701 (AUP 590) entered service in September 1936 and proved to be the forerunner of a small fleet of SE4s. Apart from the elimination of the trailing axle the mechanical specification was basically similar to that of the last batch of SE6s. Short Bros were no longer in the market for bus bodywork, having directed their efforts to aircraft production due to the deteriorating world situation, so the body for 701 was built by English Electric in the Dick Kerr works at Preston. Its shortened length meant the elimination of a row of seats, reducing the carrying

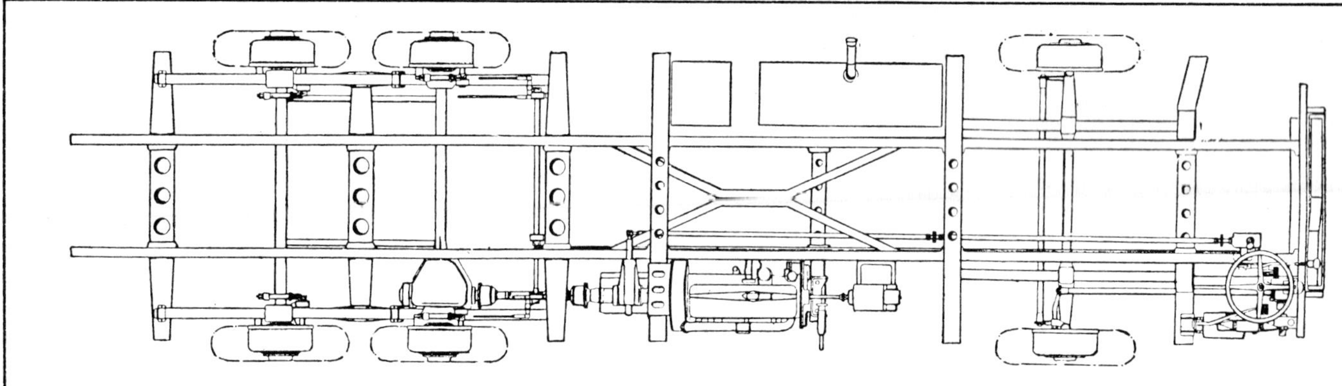

The rather pleasant rear end layout of the first standard SE6, no 604, is shown here. Notably modern body design features are the downward sweep of the side moulding and the sloping pillars, the latter being a feature which could hardly have contributed to the strength of the body structure. The hubs and wheel rings are clearly AEC-influenced.

A plan drawing of the SE6 indicates clearly the simple layout and remarkable accessibility of this highly ingenious model. The interesting bogie springing system is shown in the second diagram, including the small reaction spring to prevent excessive movement of the rocker and – in theory at least – to permit better driving adhesion.

capacity to forty. In the same year (1936) the last SE6s were built. There were only five of them, 102–3 (CN 7430–1) being a pair of coaches with Dartford-built Beadle bodies closely resembling those of the 95–100 batch, and 104–6 (FT 3903–5) Weymann-bodied saloons for the Tynemouth fleet. These latest SE6s brought the NGT chassis numbers up to 106.

One further batch of chassis was destined for construction at Bensham before the outbreak of war. Chassis 107–31 were a batch of 25 SE4s (802–26 CPT 902–26) which joined the fleet between May 1938 and the beginning of 1939. Two-axled vehicles were decided upon even though it meant a loss of seating capacity, it now being clear that the earning capacity of the four extra seats on the six-wheeler could not, on balance, justify the maintenance of the rear bogie. Right up to the time of their construction Major Hayter had been hoping for a relaxation in the ludicrous 27ft 6ins length restriction on two-axled psvs, and the SE4 was designed to a 30ft length in anticipation of this happening. Unfortunately, negotiations between the industry's representatives and the Minister of Transport to remove the anomaly collapsed and the production batch of SE4s, like their predecessor of 1936, emerged with their chassis frame shortened at the rear by 2ft 6ins. Once again composite framed 40-seater bodies were supplied by English Electric.

The 1938 batch of SE4s marked a major change from the company's former home-built vehicles in that they were diesel powered. The use of a diesel engine had become possible thanks to the introduction by AEC at the 1935 Commercial Motor Show of its medium size A172 6.6 litre engine. Designed principally for the 0862 model, Regal II, the new engine had a bore and stroke of 105mm and 130mm respectively. Northern realised that the compactness resulting from the comparatively short stroke made it suitable for the SE4 provided that the cylinders were inclined to the offside to prevent the cylinder heads interfering with the seat platform, a system copied from the AEC Q. On the SE4 the diesel engine was mounted at an angle of 30 degrees in the frame. Several major modifications had to be made to the engine, access to which was from the opposite side to that encountered on the Regal II, including an offside fuel pump. A special oil sump also had to be fitted. The A172 was an indirect injection Ricardo design, but in later life the engines were rebuilt with direct injection cylinder heads to increase efficiency. A new bell housing was made which was more rigid and substantial than the original, and it was cast locally by Parsons

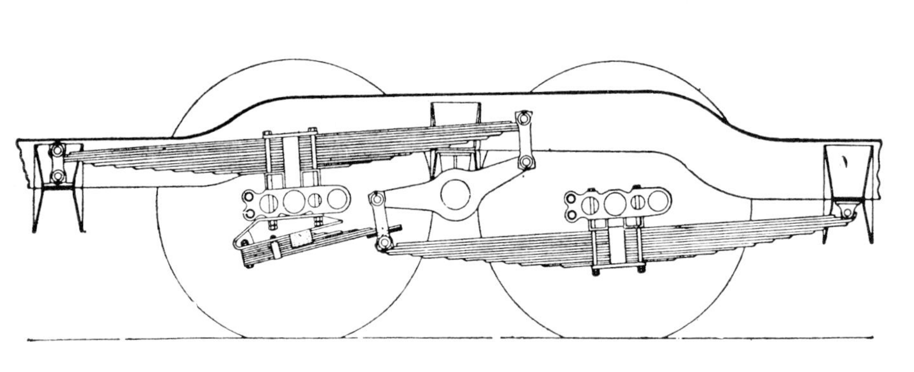

of Heddon.

The war years were a difficult time for all bus operators, who often had to show great resourcefulness when faced with the problem of finding spare parts for non-standard types such as Northern's SE4s and SE6s were. Both models performed very well through-out the war although the back axle

A view looking rearward from the front bulkhead of no 604 shows the remarkable interior layout of 44 seats, all facing forwards. The single skinned panelling, which laid bare the roof hoops, marred the overall effect and would have attracted unsightly condensation on cool days, but the seats are comfortable enough.

arrangement on the six-wheelers continued to prove troublesome at times. Early in the war Major Hayter approached Sir John Maxwell, then Regional Traffic Commissioner for the Northern Region, with a request that the trailing axle might be removed from one of the SE6s in an experiment to double the adhesion between the driving wheels and the road. Probably to the surprise of Major Hayter, permission was readily given on the basis of a twelve-month experiment. Vehicle no 604 was duly converted early in 1941, becoming, in the process, the first two-axle 44-seat single decker ever to operate in this country. As expected, the experiment was a complete success, and it was logical to expect that approval would now be forthcoming similarly to convert the 33 remaining SE6 service buses which were busily employed carrying munition and other workers essential to the war effort. However, the bureaucracy in London thought otherwise, and the Minister of War Transport refused to give his permission. He generously agreed to allow no 604 to continue operating in its rebuilt form and issued a special order no 203 on 27th January 1942 to legalise the situation.

The bus industry has produced a sprinkling of real 'characters' over the years and hopefully will continue to do so. One of these was Gordon Hayter, seen here at his desk in 1954 and looking much younger than a man on the verge of retirement. A cut-out of an SE4 single decker of his own design is by his right hand.

The six SE6 touring coaches brought a new standard of comfort and design when they were introduced onto touring work in 1935. The forward control and large front windows greatly assisted drivers in judging distances and widths, particularly when negotiating tight corners such as this one at Mousehole on the Cornish Riviera Tour.

The first SE4 – and the only one with a petrol engine – was even more modernistic in appearance than the six wheelers thanks to the streamlined and better balanced frontal appearance and the treatment given to the mudguards on its English Electric body. The sliding door across the saloon entrance is seen in the open position.

The war years saw the commencement of a major modification programme on the SE6s. Starting in1943, the replacement of petrol engines in all the saloons (including the prototype four-wheeler no 701) by diesel units got under way. The engines concerned were AEC units very similar to the A172 but modified for use in the Matilda tank, and numbers of them became available because of developments in tank design which had made the Matilda obsolete. The engines came in pairs and were classified A183 and A184, according to whether the auxiliaries were on the left or the right hand side. Those with nearside mounted units were placed into SOS chassis but their partners with offside mounted units, which would have had little general application

For fair weather touring on the SE6s, the roll-back canvas hood proved a great boon, but more often than not the weather was less than brilliant and the hood remained closed, and in view of the shortage of luggage space and lack of body rigidity their retention could not be justified. One of the coaches is seen just south of Exeter in the days before a fixed roof was fitted.

for psv work, were earmarked for the side-engined vehicles. The petrol to oil conversions were carried out over a period of years up to 1947, engines being converted prior to installation to direct injection in the same manner as those on the SE4s. The engines were rather larger than the old Hercules units and a shallow box had to be constructed into the saloon floor to accommodate the tops of the cylinder heads, but otherwise their installation was a comparatively simple operation.

The eight coaches remained petrol-engined and so did no 586, the 1933 prototype, which was withdrawn from service in 1945 and ended life as a static caravan. In 1946 the eight Tynemouth SE6s were transferred to the parent fleet in which they received fleet numbers 1153–60 (FT 3478–82, 3903–5). The side-engined fleet continued to serve the company well throughout the early years of post-war revival and it was

Rebuilding of the touring coaches resulted in a big change in their appearance, especially as a large area of light colouring was incorporated in the livery, a feature first introduced on the two Beadle-bodied machines.

not until 1952 that any withdrawals took place. Even the coaches resumed a fully active life back on extended tour work despite their increasing age. The author remembers inspecting one at Llanberis in the

The 1938/9 production batch of diesel engined SE4s took streamlining yet another stage further with the downward sweep of the last side windows but the overall effect was, if anything, over-fussy. The seats fitted to the SE4s were more utilitarian and less comfortable in appearance than those on the earlier side engined vehicles.

Quite apart from the side-engined layout actually adopted in practice by Gordon Hayter were his ideas for rear-engined chassis. Though not put into production by NGT these 1934 sketches make interesting study in the light of future trends.

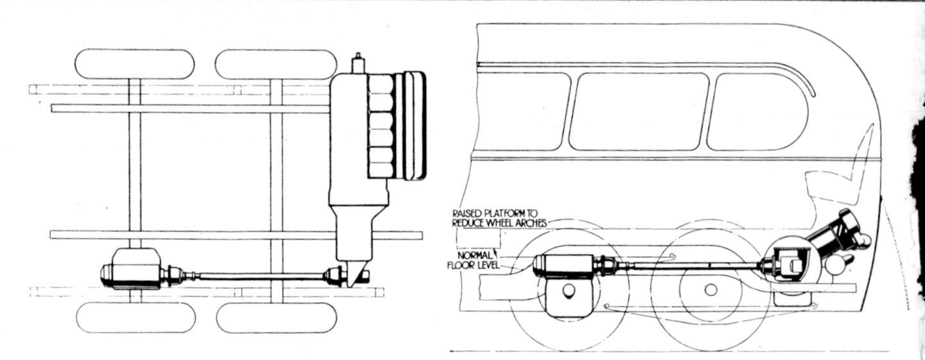

early nineteen-fifties and even then it appeared more sumptuous, impressive and modern looking than most of the new touring coaches that were around at the time.

Mass withdrawals took place in 1954, when the side-engined vehicles were finally eliminated from the fleet with the possible exception of an odd one or two that may have soldiered on for a few weeks into 1955. It might have been expected that this would be the end of the road for such non-standard vehicles, but their condition was still fairly good and several were sold to a London dealer from whom a few passed into the hands of small coach operators or building contractors for a further short spell of service. The only known survivor today is no 604, the SE6 which became a four-wheeler back in 1941. In December 1954, at the end of its service career, it was presented by Northern to the British Transport Commission for its collection of historic vehicles, being the first bus from outside London to join the collection in the then unopened Clapham Museum. A small ceremony took place at Bensham on 2nd December when Gordon Hayter handed the bus over to the BTC's curator, John H Scholes. The framed Ministry of War Transport Order of 1942 was handed over with it.

Throughout the war years and for some time afterwards Northern abandoned the concept of manufacturing its own vehicles. The excellent if some-what austere Guy Arab arrived on the scene and Hayter became firmly wedded to these vehicles both during the war and after it for most new vehicle requirements. However, by 1950 the company had returned to the drawing board with another new chassis of its own design. Spurred on by the rising capital outlay required on new vehicles and the need for economy to keep fares as low as possible, an austere single deck saloon bus was devised which made use of second-hand components wherever possible. A prototype was built in 1951 in which the company contrived to squeeze 43 seats into a front-engined vehicle of 30ft length and 8ft width. The chassis frame was an almost straight design which was at normal height just behind the front axle but thereafter swept straight upwards to give clearance over the back axle, rearward from the centre of which it again became horizontal. Its side members were fabricated from sections (four on each side) which were made of $\frac{1}{4}$in mild steel at the Redheugh Iron & Steel Company's works in Gateshead; they were butt welded and provided with fish plates to give added strength. The running units were removed from a Regal II chassis of 1936 vintage, one of a batch of 25 Weymann-bodied saloons whose with-

drawal commenced in 1951, but the engine used was an AEC 7.7 as against the smaller one of the Regal II. In order to enable the passenger saloon to be as long as possible, the engine compartment was reduced from the normal 4ft $5\frac{1}{4}$ins to 3ft $10\frac{7}{8}$ins by removing the water pump from the front of the engine and driving it instead from the tail end of the dynamo.

The complete chassis weighed 4 tons and a composite body was constructed which, at just over 2 tons, resulted in an unladen weight for the complete 43-seater of 6 tons 0 cwt 3 qr. The body was built at Chester-le-Street by the Picktree Coach & Engineering Co Ltd, an NGT subsidiary which had carried out bus body construction on the company's premises since just before the Second World War. Extremely ugly externally, and incredibly spartan internally, the body was designed for mass movement

No 604, the first 'production' side engined saloon, in its second guise as a four wheeler, a form to which all the others would have been converted had bureaucracy not stepped in to decree otherwise. The photograph was taken at Bensham on the day of its handing over ceremony to the British Transport Commission.

The comfort and spaciousness of the floral moquette seating can be seen in this photograph of an SE6 interior taken just after rebuilding and used for chart room booking purposes.

The 1951 lightweight saloon, no 1402, in a specially posed shot just after completion of its Picktree body and before its unladen weight has been ascertained. The raised window level at the rear of the saloon seems an unnecessary complication in a body that was otherwise built in as cheap and spartan a way as possible.

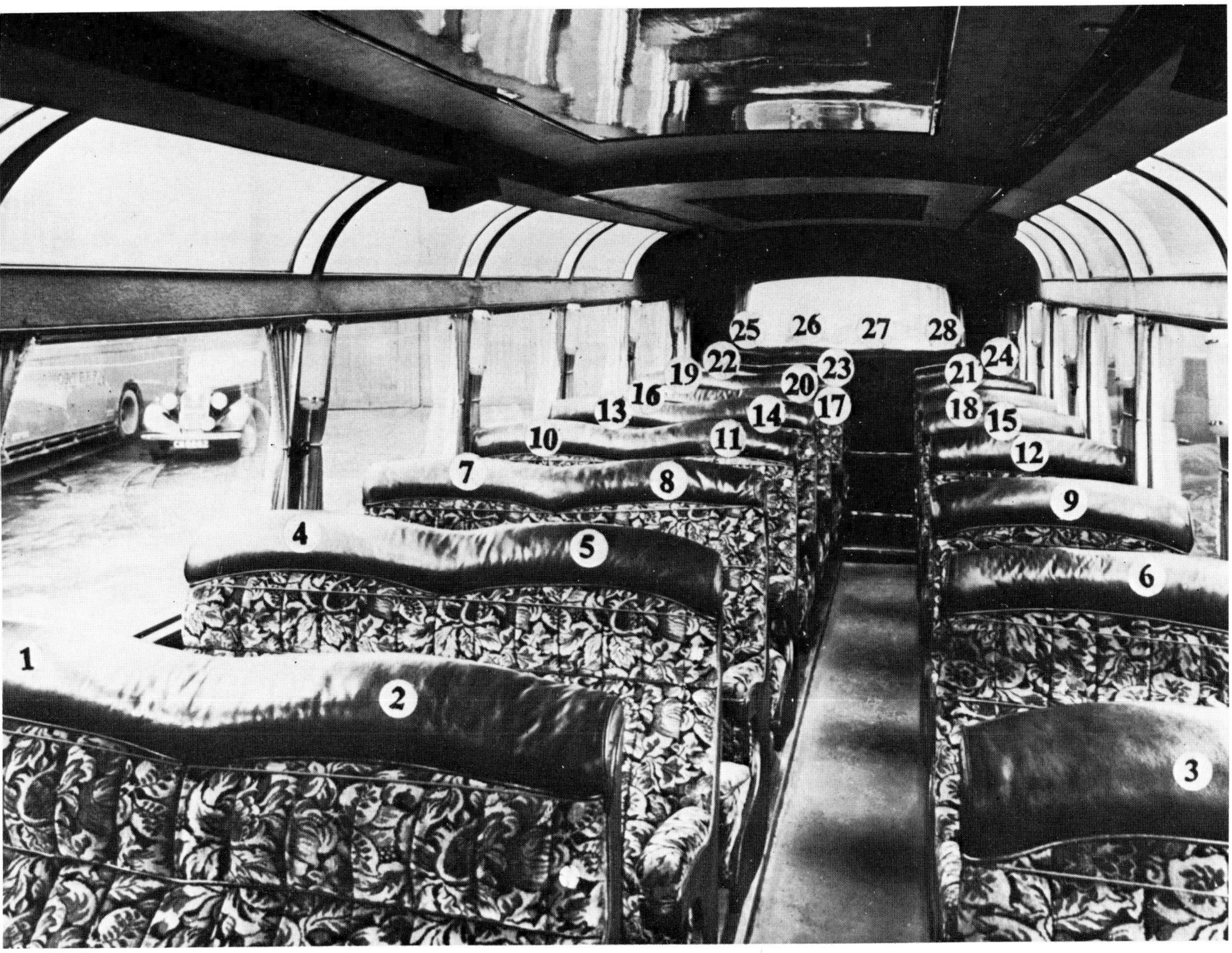

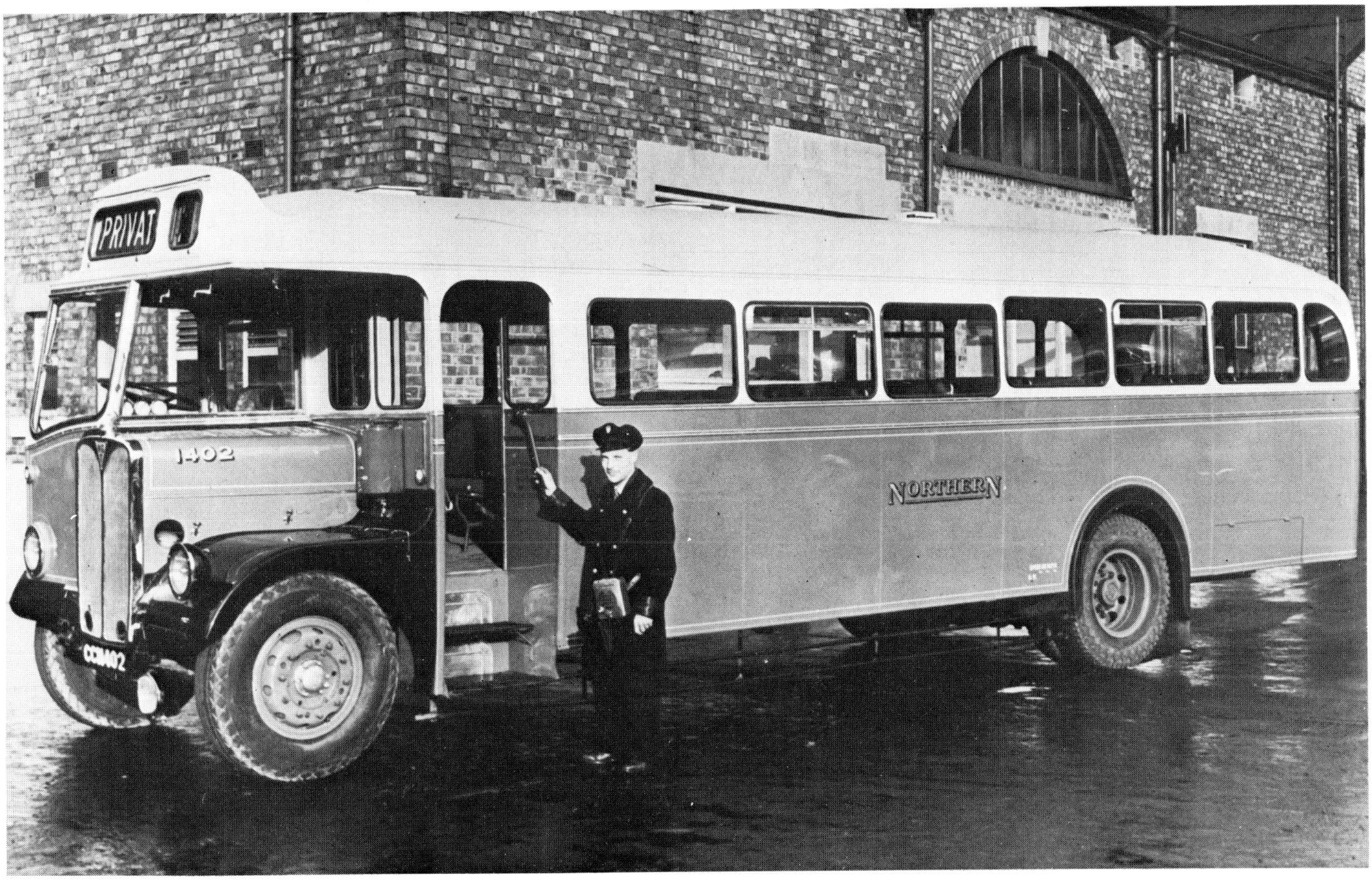

PRIVAT
1402
NORTHERN

The twenty-four touring coaches extensively rebuilt out of earlier vehicles in 1951–3 embodied a number of small differences in bodywork from batch to batch. No 1459 was one of the 1952 output. They all lacked character and a definitive sense of style, and were by no means in the same class as the SE6s which they helped to replace, especially in terms of passenger comfort where 35 seats were squeezed into a space occupied by 28 on the six-wheelers.

of miners and other groups of workers over short distances where comfort was not of paramount importance. A capacity of 43 was achieved by adopting a seat spacing of 2ft 3⅜ins – which was held to be adequate provided that the padding at the top of the seat back was kept to a minimum – and included a rearward-facing seat for two backing onto the front bulkhead. A neat feature in an otherwise depressingly utilitarian design was the nearside front wing assembly which was hinged to give quick access to the fuel pump, water pump and dynamo.

The new vehicle, known as an AEC-NGT, entered service in 1951 as fleet number 1402 (CCN 402). It was placed into service experimentally and by April 1952 had notched up some 20,000 miles without incident. This was sufficiently promising to

encourage the production of further vehicles of the same type, and two years later saw the arrival of 1467–78 (DCN 67–78). The thirteen-strong class was often referred to by the unflattering title of 'kipper boxes' but they served reasonably well for some years and, with only one exception, there was – surprisingly, perhaps – never any trouble at all at any of their welded chassis joints.

The chassis numbers allotted to the lightweight saloons were 133, 160–171. The intermediate and subsequent numbers (132, 134–59, 172–4) were given to vehicles which were not, strictly speaking, constructed by Northern but were heavily rebuilt at Bensham. Twenty-four vehicles were involved: 1368–76 (CCN 368–76) and 1388 (BCN 388) of 1951; 1404, 1457–66 (CCN 404, 677–86) of 1952; and 1493–5 (DCN 93–5) of 1953, and they were reconstructions to dimensions of 30ft × 8ft of pre-war AEC Regals of the standard 7.7 powered variety with preselector transmission and fluid flywheels. To obtain the extra length, a 1ft 3ins section was inserted just behind the front axle and as this increased the distance between the fluid flywheel and the gearbox the connecting tube had to be split and a supporting bearing fitted in the tubular crossmember. The tail end of the chassis frame was lopped off and replaced by a swept-down extension to

make a rear luggage boot possible, and the gear selector lever was re-sited from its normal position on the floor to the steering column to give added space for engine insulation. Apart from these alterations, and the flexible mounting of the engine, the chassis complied with their original AEC design. The vehicles were intended for extended tours work, and new fully-fronted Picktree coach bodies were fitted which seated 35 passengers in considerably less comfort than the 28-seater SE6s whose lives were now coming towards an end.

Colonel Hayter retired at the end of 1954, and it might have been expected that his departure would see the end of Northern's enterprise. Indeed, very little actually happened for many years. However, though hardly in the 'vintage' era, the story would not be complete without mention of two very unusual reconstructions of 1972. By this time the concept of the one-man-operated double decker was universally accepted, and the mechanical problems associated with the rear-engined buses theoretically best suited to this type of work were a cause of consternation. Throughout the country rear-engined double deckers were proving less satisfactory than the traditional front-engined models. Under its Chief Engineer, Mr D A Cox, Northern decided to tackle the problem by taking a front-engined Leyland

Titan PD3 and rebuilding it to a configuration suitable for one-man operation. Leyland no 49 (NNL 49), a 1958 bus of the conventional crew-operated type with open rear platform, was taken from the subsidiary Tyneside fleet into the Bensham works and was stipped right down, finally to emerge with its appearance radically altered. The driver's position was moved rearwards by about 2ft 6ins to place it almost opposite a single width entrance door, behind which was an exit twice its width. The body was pushed back at the front end to the new windscreen level, thus producing the novel result of a normal control double decker. The old rear staircase and platform were removed and the back filled in, and a new forward ascending staircase installed immediately behind the driver. Ahead of the driver's position a Routemaster-type bonnet and wing assembly was installed, though double sided, and alterations to the mechanical specification included a Routemaster-type semi-automatic epicyclic transmission in place of the Leyland synchromesh gearbox. The body, which started life as a standard Metro Cammell Orion type, ended up bearing little resemblance to its original shape. It was refitted and retrimmed throughout, and was repainted externally to a new style of livery, bearing prominently between decks the name 'Tynesider'.

When it emerged from Bensham, the vehicle bore a new fleet number (3000) and registration number (MCN 30 K) and must have appeared to the casual observer as a completely new if somewhat curiously shaped vehicle. It was scheduled to start operation from Gateshead depot, passing later to Wallsend and Jarrow. According to the company's early publicity, the Tynesider was a great success and very popular with crews, but this was not really the case. The extensive and costly rebuilding had completely altered the weight distribution and handling characteristics and the vehicle was not at all pleasant to drive. The steering proved to be exceptionally heavy and staff opposition to its use quickly built up at certain depots.

Following hot on the heels of the Tynesider came the Wearsider, which was a less exotic variation on the same theme. In this instance the vehicle selected was one of the 51 chassisless Park Royal Routemasters which were giving excellent service on some of Northern's trunk routes but which were completely unsuitable for one-man operation. No 2085 (RCN 685) was given part of the treatment meted out to the Tynesider. The driver's position was placed further back, but not quite so far, resulting in a semi-forward control layout. The staircase also had to be moved rearwards by an equivalent amount, but the whole of the near-

The photograph of the 1951 prototype chassis shows the simple frame and suspension arrangements and the reconditioned AEC axles and 7.7 engine.

The Tynesider was one of the weirdest looking double deck creations for many years, and it is a pity that it failed to achieve the success expected of it. It is seen at the company's Washington depôt where the full oddity of its shape can be seen from a nearside view.

A Routemaster with a difference! The Wearsider was by no means as revolutionary in appearance as the Tynesider but its compromise design made it aesthetically much less pleasing due to the ugly overhang of the front upper deck.

side of the bus remained substantially the same as it was previously, as did most of the main upper deck structure. The resultant appearance was something of a hotch-potch, the normal good looks of the Routemaster being completely destroyed by the massive overhang of the upper deck forward of the windscreen. It was announced at the time that the whole Wearsider conversion had cost about £1250 and that if reaction from staff and public was favourable – as seemed likely – the remaining fifty Routemasters would be similarly dealt with. They never were!

Gerald Nowell
BUS OPERATOR EXTRAORDINARY

The transport industry has created a number of really dynamic men, but few can have had such success in so many different operations, nor have worked so amicably for so many managements as well as for himself as the late Gerald Nowell. CHRIS TAYLOR looks at the fascinating and varied career of a busman extraordinary.

GERALD Nowell's span of working life in the industry was only from 1923 until 1951 and he is now largely forgotten, but in his time he created two passenger concerns, built up a large private hire business, operated and consolidated a major express undertaking, and finally took over top management of a large independent concern.

Gerald Nowell began his career in London when, at the age of 25, he became a 'pirate' busman in the cut-and-thrust days before the London Traffic Act which came into force early in 1925 to stifle competition and protect the combine. He had already led a varied career prior to this, having served in the latter part of the war as a lorry driver in the RASC and later joining the RNVR. He had enjoyed a public school education – at St Paul's,

Hammersmith – and this, no doubt, helped him into the Foreign Office when his war service came to an end. Unable to settle down to a career in

The opening of the Welsh Midnight Express in March 1929 was a great event for GWE. Star of the ceremony at the inaugural run was one of the new Leyland Tigers which was christened in traditional manner with a bottle of champagne before setting off from London.

Photographs of Haywood & Nowell's Orange buses on London service are extremely rare. This one depicts Orange no 10, the little Dennis 2½ tonner taken over from Dauntless in March 1926 and sporting orange and black livery. It was pictured at Finsbury Park in July 1927, two months after the Orange became an LGOC subsidiary, and it carries the latter's fleet number and running code plates.

Great Western Express commenced operation in October 1928 with a trio of Tilling-Stevens Expresses bodied by Dodson as very comfortable 20-seaters. In this posed shot the route running boards on the roof luggage rack can be seen reading *London–Henley–Oxford–Burford–Cheltenham–Gloucester–Newport–Cardiff.*

from the bus with a partial refund of their fare so that it could change its line of route, that got many of the independents a bad name and resulted in the London Traffic Act which prohibited such behaviour. Haywood & Nowell prospered and soon there was enough money in the kitty to buy a second bus and in February 1924 XR 4129, another Leyland, was delivered, ready to be licensed on the first of the next month. The partners continued to work on the buses themselves until they could afford to employ other men and they finally gave up to concentrate on general management when their third vehicle was purchased in September 1924.

XU 8727 was a Dennis, and so was XW 473 which followed it less than a month later. The choice of chassis was probably influenced by the fact that Dennis were then asking £150 less per vehicle than Leyland. June 1925 saw the delivery of bus no 5, YK 3657, which marked a return to Leyland. All five chassis in the fleet bore identical bodies by Dodson, from whom they had been bought on hire purchase. In addition to the buses and the tobacco business, Haywood & Nowell had their fingers in other pies at this stage. They advertised cars for hire, were agents for the Royal Insurance Co Ltd and others, supplied motor accessories and tyres, and were agents for the 'Empire' automatic petrol economiser, a gadget made by the New Motor Speciality Co Ltd. Their trading address was 119 Alexandria Road, St John's Wood – Haywood's home.

The business was incorporated as a limited company under the title of Haywood & Nowell Ltd on 31st July 1925 with a nominal capital of £4000 and registered office at the Victoria Yard, which was the colloquial title of the BB Motor Works in Boundary Road. Haywood and Nowell were the first directors and they allotted themselves 1750 shares at £1 each. The limited company took over operation of the buses on 31st August, and on 25th October a man named Thomas Ernest Huntley was appointed to manage the business and given the title Managing Director, although his shareholding was purely nominal.

In January 1926 buses 6 and 7 were

the civil service, the young Nowell left to join Lever Brothers' Advertising department, in which he worked for a while in Africa, and it was whilst with Lever Brothers that he met his future business partner. George Barton Haywood, three years Nowell's senior, was another ex-public schoolboy who had a banking background and a distinguished army service from which he had been invalided out with the rank of captain.

The two first ventured into business together in 1922 as Haywood & Nowell by obtaining a licence to deal in cigarettes and tobacco and a fairly substantial trade was built up in the sale of hand-made cigarettes. It is a far cry from selling tobacco to running buses, but Haywood & Nowell were convinced that the two trades could be carried on successfully side by side, and went on to prove they were right. They ventured into the bus business with the purchase of a new Leyland

XP 4355, which was licensed on 1st November 1923. It was a typical London-type open top, solid tyred, bonneted double decker which soon became a regular feature of the London scene, often with Haywood at the wheel and Nowell collecting fares, and it bore a distinctive livery of orange and cream and proudly displayed 'The Orange Service' on each side.

The Orange bus was stabled overnight at the BB Motor Works in Boundary Road, St John's Wood, being one of several independent buses for which the owner, Arthur Bell Hewitt, provided accommodation, others being the Rapid, Western and Paragon. During the day it worked on a whole variety of lucrative central London routes, following the typical independent pattern of the time by switching from service to service according to wherever trade was busiest. It was this constant changing about which often resulted in passengers being ejected

The second delivery of vehicles to Great Western Express, in February 1929, consisted of three TS2 type Leyland Tiger 22-seaters. Again Dodson provided the bodies. The route indicates that the service has now pressed on westwards to Swansea by way of Bridgend and Neath.

One of the Leyland Tigers was in service for only about six months when its body was destroyed by fire. Dodson provided a 26-seater replacement which was rather taller and more rounded in appearance than the original. The fleet number 12 is carried on the autovac tank, but it is not known how this was arrived at as the GWE fleet never grew beyond six units.

ordered from Dodson, and in the following month nos 8 and 9 were also contracted for. Unlike their fore-runners, the new buses were pneumatic tyred single deckers with chassis by Dennis. They were intended for a new route, 550, which the company intended to pioneer between Finsbury Park and Islington (Chapel Street). Fresh capital was required for this dramatic expansion of the business from five to nine buses and this was provided by Arthur Bell Hewitt, who took a major shareholding in the business and also became a director. The single deckers were quickly delivered. YM 5154/5 came during the same month in which they were ordered and YM 9971/2 arrived at the beginning of March 1926. They were normal control 25-seaters which proved to be reasonably reliable although faulty metal in the con-rods caused early troubles and the fan drive soon had to be converted from flat to whittle belting. These buses introduced a new colour scheme. Instead of the attractive orange and cream, they bore an even more striking combination of orange and black. Their owners must have been pleased with the result as they duly repainted their double deckers orange and black also.

Two other operators arranged to run alongside the Orange fleet on route 550, providing one vehicle apiece. YM 6965/6 were single deckers identical to the Orange vehicles and were owned by A J R Martin (who ran as Nulli Secundus) and the Farewell Omnibus Co Ltd (Dauntless) respectively. Both were licensed on 1st February 1926 but on 25th March they passed to Orange, their owners presumably having quickly become disillusioned with route 550 which was slow to pick up at first.

In October 1926 the company ordered from Dodson its last new bus, a pneumatic tyred Dennis E type single decker. This 30-seater entered service towards the end of November, but by now the firm was getting into trouble. December 1926 was a very bleak month as police stops were placed on no fewer than six out of the twelve strong fleet, and nos 2, 4, 7, 8, 9 and 11 had to be taken out of service for repair. The 550 must have been badly hit

with the non-availability of four out of the seven single deckers. Apparently the company had expanded beyond its capacity to maintain the fleet in good condition. The writing was on the wall, and 1927 turned out to be the last year of independent operation by Haywood & Nowell Ltd. At a meeting at 55 Broadway on 16th May the entire share capital of the company was purchased by General. Barton Haywood and Gerald Nowell were temporarily appointed joint managers to continue operations from St John's Wood for the time being on the LGOC's behalf. They continued to train, clothe and supervise their men and, apart from using LGOC tickets from about the end of May, there was little apparent evidence to show that the business had changed hands. This arrangement continued until 4th July when the LGOC took over the operations itself, and it continued to maintain Orange as a subsidiary until 1st January 1928.

The takeover of the business by General was even reported in *The Daily Mail* of 24th May under the headline 'Omnibus Romance – Fortunes for two young city men'. In addition to the usual story about how the LGOC was offering £2500 each for the vehicles, there was an interesting little note: '*They gave up positions in a large city firm to start an omnibus service. Beginning with one vehicle they acted in turn as conductor. Often one would be returning home in the bus in evening dress while the other was collecting tickets in uniform*'.

Following the LGOC takeover of the Orange operation, Barton Haywood left the bus industry, but for Gerald Nowell buswork was now in the blood and he was soon to the forefront once again. On 30th July 1928 he formed the Great Western Express Company Ltd, a name which reminds us of the present cult for naming drinks, van hire, etc, after the old Great Western Railway. The first board meeting was held in August 1928 with Gerald Nowell and his wife present, when shares were allocated between the two of them. Nowell intended to run a fast, regular service between London and South Wales, for which three Tilling-Stevens B10A2 Expresses with forward control were delivered in October 1928. The bodies, seating only 20, were built by Christopher Dodson, who probably put up some of the finance. They had armchair type seats upholstered in brown antique furniture hide, the backs of them having folding tables. There was also a lavatory compartment at the rear which included a pol-

Samuelson's Saloon Coaches came into the Red & White fold in September 1931 but only two modern AEC Regals were acquired, both carrying Scammell & Nephew bodies. One of these is seen displaying the route board for Samuelson's London–Liverpool run.

An interesting line-up of Red & White vehicles shortly after the GWE takeover shows how varied the fleet was at the time. From left to right can be seen a Northern Counties bodied Albion Valliant of 1933, an ex-GWE Tilling Stevens Express, a 1928 Petty bodied AJS Pilot, another ex-GWE Tilling, and two other Albions of various vintage.

ished walnut wash-hand basin. The vehicle livery was very tasteful, having lower panels in crimson lake, upper in French grey, with a waistband of chrome yellow separating them The wings and wheels were also painted French grey.

The service chosen was from London to Cardiff, a route length of about 170 miles, travelling by way of Oxford, Cheltenham, Gloucester and Monmouth. When he started the service in October 1928 Nowell was not the only operator on the South Wales run. Over a year earlier, in April 1927, another former London bus operator, Finlay & Hoiland (who had run the Gleaner bus) started a service which traded as Rural England Motor Coaches Ltd. In August 1928 this firm made the most odd agreement with a group of companies which later became Red & White Services Ltd and included the Watts family (of Watts Factors), Guy Bown and T J Jones (of Griffin, Brynmawr), Ralph Williams, etc, all of whom later formed the United Transport concern that is still with us today. This agreement was supposed to help both Rural England and the group, but in effect gave the group time to purchase a fleet of coaches and to gain a foothold which they did not previously have. For a time their vehicles

were run in the brown livery of Rural England, but for some reason the two operators fell out early in 1929 and went their separate ways. Rural England, left without enough vehicles, was voluntarily liquidated in January 1930. Red & White had to find themselves a new timetable cover as it showed one of Rural England's Tilling-Stevens; they, of course, went from strength to strength and became Great Western Express' greatest competitor.

Another operator on the route was Cook's Safety Coaches Ltd, who began just ahead of Great Western Express in July 1928 with a fleet of De Dion Bouton coaches. This firm also ran to Brighton, Portsmouth and other seaside resorts, but later concentrated on the South Wales road. However, at the end of 1929 a Receiver was appointed as money was owed to Johnson Neal Ltd, the main De Dion Bouton dealers, and the service was taken over by Queen Line Coastal Coaches, sometimes being called Cook's Queen Line Service.

The origins of Queen Line are rather unusual. In October 1928 a firm called Baldock Motor Transport began a service from Biggleswade and Baldock to London whilst Queen Line began a service from York and Hull to London. Both were financially associated

with Johnson Neal so all their early vehicles were De Dion JE2s, as were Cook's. Further new Queen Line services were commenced to Llandudno (Easter 1929), Ilfracombe (June 1929) and later during 1929 to Worthing, Bognor, Clacton, Ramsgate and Bexhill. All except the Llandudno one were suspended at the end of the year. However, the Cook's service to South Wales was taken over in October 1929 because of the Johnson Neal connection, even though the liquidator of Cook's did not want local councils to transfer the licences in the interest of creditors. In April 1930 Queen Line and Baldock Motor Transport were linked under the unwieldy title of Queen Line Coaches & Baldock Motor Transport Ltd, but at the end of 1930 the South Wales service was sold to A T Morse.

So much for the competition. Gerald Nowell had not been idle, as on 2nd March 1929 an increased service was started using three new Leyland Tiger TS2 22-seaters, again with Dodson bodies. This model had a great deal more power than the Tilling Stevens Express which, though totally reliable, had not lived up to its name. Included in the new schedules was a service called the 'Welsh Midnight', leaving London at 12 midnight. The inaugural run was given a proper send-off by two famous stage personalities of the time, sisters Renée and Billie Houston, using a bottle of champagne on the radiator. This attention to publicity by Nowell made sure that all was reported in the commercial press of the time. The passengers must have been a strong breed as the overnight run took $7\frac{1}{2}$ hours. The fare, however, was only 28/- (£1.40) return. A rather odd service connection was given from Cardiff in conjunction with P & A Campbell's White Funnel steamers to Weston-super-Mare, Ilfracombe and Minehead across the Bristol Channel, hardly of any use for London travellers but of possible convenience for those from intermediate points.

Problems were, however, looming on the horizon. Up to now the South Wales local councils had considered express services not to be worth licensing but towards the end of 1929, due to the number of coaches and operators running and requesting services,

the Cardiff City Council decided to refuse all licences. At the subsequent enquiry Gerald Nowell and John Watts (of Red & White) both had to go before the Council. Their paths were subsequently to cross many times. The police tried hard to prove that Great Western Express was operating illegally, but were unsuccessful in their efforts, and the company was duly re-licensed. GWE soon opened a garage in Cardiff, together with a booking agency, and Gerald Nowell also began a new agency in London called The General Travel Agency.

Expansion of services to Swansea took place in October 1929, and in 1930 competition with the Red & White group began in earnest when services reached out into the South Wales valleys. A major problem lay in obtaining licences from all the small councils with whom the Red & White group were very friendly. At a Ministry of Transport enquiry at Swansea it was asked whether a service taking 12½ hours running time to London was popular, and this popularity had to be proved. The greatest problems over licences took place in Abergavenny, Tredegar and Brynmawr where the battle became very personal with threats of libel being bandied about. Red & White, always waiting for a chance to fight GWE, gave evidence at the MOT enquiries in support of the councils, completely impartially of course! GWE eventually got their own back as they obtained the necessary licences and began approaching Red & White agents in the Rhondda valley (agent being a rather posh name for what were local shops that sold tickets).

An even bigger fight lay ahead. The Road Traffic Act had come into effect in 1931 and a battle took place between Red & White, Great Western Express and Black & White for the prime South Wales routes. There were only two other small operators on the scene, Cliff's and London & South Wales Express, who later merged.

GWE did not obtain all the licences that it asked for, appealed and lost against the licences granted to Red & White and Black & White. The combined effect of not having these licences, the competition from other operators with larger reserves, the depression, and restrictions that the Traffic Commissioners imposed caused financial losses. Even Red & White, with all its financial backing, lost heavily on the long distance operations and this was instrumental, in time, in the formation of Associated Motorways in order to produce reductions in mileages and vehicles. GWE's

fortunes declined rapidly, and Nowell did not have the cash reserves to withstand the continuing pressure. Christopher Dodson became the guarantor for the bank in May 1932 whilst Gerald Nowell looked around for a buyer for the business. He offered it to both Red & White and Black & White. The former moved fastest and took over the services at midnight on 30th June 1932. The deal was 9,000 fully paid Red & White shares for 1,000 GWE of £1 each and all liabilities paid. The General Travel Agency was also taken over. The licences could not be transferred immediately so the GWE company continued under the control of Red & White until October 1932. Full coordination was quickly put into effect with Black & White, allowing for a considerable reduction in the service especially in winter months. This had the unfortunate effect of placing yet more drivers on the dole at a time when jobs were very scarce.

Gerald Nowell stayed on with Red & White to become a director with specific responsibility for the London end of its operations. The company

had begun its association with private hire work in London when it took over control of Samuelsons Saloon Coaches in September 1931. The former principals of this firm, W H Cook and S H Hole, were also one-time London bus operators trading as Dominion and A1. Hole had purchased the assets of Samuelsons back in 1922 and in August 1928 had formed it into a limited company as Samuelson New Transport Ltd.

From Samuelsons, Red & White took over only two AEC Regals out of the entire fleet, not wanting the remainder. Other businesses acquired by Red & White were MacShanes in December 1932 and All British Travels in January 1933, and these probably also brought in some more private hire work in addition to their regular long distance services. Gerald Nowell concentrated on this and built up a large business, one of the most interesting aspects being its association with film transport. A 24-hour service was operated and practically all this form of work was captured in London by Red & White. By 1936 there were fourteen

film producing concerns around the capital, and Red & White had twelve coaches working more or less full time throughout the year on these contracts. They sometimes had to turn out as many as 30 coaches in one night. This type of work required a great deal of coordination between the office and the drivers with regard to hours of driving, relief drivers being used when on location. Red & White must have been very pleased with their new director.

The Red & White success story was soon to be followed by a similar success with the acquired firm of Blue Belle. The association between the two began in January 1934 when it was arranged for Red & White and Black & White vehicles to garage at Blue Belle's London Terminal Coach Station for £300 a year. Blue Belle were probably very grateful for this income as the station must have looked very empty at this time, many of its former client companies having either sold out to railway-associated concerns or faded away through lack of income. Blue Belle was offered for sale in June 1934, but Red & White were not in a position to buy at the time, due mostly to losses on their MacShanes operations in Liverpool. G Scammell & Nephew arranged to take control of the firm, but this lasted only a short while before Blue Belle reverted to its original ownership. It was not until 1936 that negotiations with Red & White began in earnest. In November 1936 Blue Belle was offered £12,750 plus £5,000 directors' compensation and this was acceptable to them. A new company was formed entitled Blue Belle Coaching Services Ltd, to which all vehicles and licences were transferred. The six executive directors of Red & White became directors along with Gerald Nowell.

There was no hope of the London Terminal Station trading profitably as a coach station and it was put up for auction in February 1937, but a private deal was arranged with Mr Bown (a director of Red & White) and Gerald Nowell, who purchased it for £57,500. As soon as the deposit was paid, associated companies in other spheres of transport began to move into the station, the first being Mechanisation Ltd with 20 vehicles, then W Baker & Sons, a haulage concern, a platform for loading goods being built for this purpose. Private cars were also being garaged at the Terminal Station and great efforts were made to advertise this service in the trade press. All British Carriers, another transport firm owned by the executive directors of Red & White, took up possession of part of the station in October 1937, so the place must have started to look a bit more busy. With the garaging of 25 *News Chronicle* vehicles the whole of the garage space was finally taken, not a bad result for a year's work by Gerald Nowell.

To diversify, Gerald Nowell proposed that taxicabs should be operated and six were ordered from Mann & Overton at £395 each. These were delivered in December 1937 when operations began. A proposal was made by Mr Nowell to operate coaches on the London streets during a bus strike in May 1937 but the other directors put a stop to this idea.

As could be expected, with Red & White's expertise with oil engined vehicles it was not long before 6LW Gardner engines were ordered for fitting into the six Blue Belle Cruisers (AEC Regal observation coaches). In addition, three Albion/Duple coaches were ordered, a continuation of Red & White's standard purchasing policy, and these were also of the raised-deck, observation type which had become something of a Blue Belle trademark. One of these vehicles was shown at the Earls Court exhibition.

There were, however, problems with the service licences of Blue Belle which resulted in 48 objections to their renewal in January 1938. Certain excursions and tours were disallowed and other licences altered. The Traffic Manager in London was thereupon sacked. To obtain better control of their London operations the Red & White fleet in London was transferred to Blue Belle, all under the management of Gerald Nowell. This scheme was carried out from September 1938 after which Red & White no longer operated its own coach services in London, which was perhaps a pity after so much success had been achieved in such a comparatively short time.

Thanks to the efforts of Gerald Nowell, private hire work continued to run at a high level, such as the Australian Government tour in 1939 and a contract to operate between Olympia and Earls Court for the British Industries Fair. But then war intervened; the depôt was closed and only a skeleton staff remained. Gerald Nowell's job appeared to be in the balance, but as soon as the initial shock of war had worn off, business was being obtained again. London Transport entered into an agreement to garage 50 surplus

Private hire played an important part in Blue Belle's work, and Gerald Nowell worked hard to foster this side of its activities even further once it came under his control. Three of the distinctive observation AEC Regals of 1933 are seen on a private outing along with the company's only Bedford which had originated as a van but had been rebodied by Duple as a coach in 1934.

A Duple-bodied Albion 6LW of 1937 is seen on one of the first trips to the Continent organised by Gerald Nowell. The method of lifting the vehicle on board ship at Dover illustrates one of the difficulties involved in sending coaches abroad at the time.

buses at the Terminal Station at 4s 6d per vehicle per week from February 1940. Gates and wire fences were erected inside the station to prevent pilfering.

Gerald Nowell arranged for the 1940 season to operate at 75% of the 1939 level. Unfortunately, a scheme for coordination of services with other London operators was rather oddly turned down. However, the 'phoney war' was coming to an end. In July 1940 thirteen of Blue Belle's vehicles were requisitioned by the military authorities and all coastal services except Brighton closed down. Fuel was becoming in short supply. In November 1940 three incendiary bombs fell on the coach station and a number of London Transport vehicles were burnt, in addition to which all the windows on the forecourt were blown out.

But by now Gerald Nowell had departed from the scene, having accepted a commission in the RAOC in October 1940.

It was soon decided to sell the taxicabs and to close down the London operations. All the contracts in London had expired and vehicles were urgently required in South Wales by Red & White. In March 1941 almost the whole of the garage space was let to London Transport, and not a moment too soon. In May it was severely damaged and the roof completely demolished. Only the parts used by long distance coaches and by All British Carriers were repaired.

John Watts was soon thinking about post-war operations, and in late 1942 began negotiating with Mr French of United Services (a long-standing coach and haulage proprietor). The proposals also quickly brought in Timpsons, the idea being to have a large London based coach operation consisting of all three operators. The

AEC vehicles of Timpsons were to be hired to the Red & White group which still required vehicles, but unfortunately negotiations broke down and in 1944 Alexander Timpson died and the firm was sold to the BET. If this had not happened, we may have seen a very large London fleet of combined operators on the post-war scene. The end result of these negotiations was that Blue Belle, United Services and Orange Luxury Coaches (the London subsidiary of Keith & Boyle Ltd, which was jointly owned by Red & White, United Transport and United Services) became financially linked. Blue Belle had been reformed with various original and secondhand AEC Regals and was finally sold to United Services in August 1945.

Before passing on to the post-war scene, it should be mentioned that Gerald Nowell became associated with other interests of the Red & White directors. His former travel agency at 9 Great Newport Street was taken over by Red & White and this took over the London control of Red & White and Samuelson bookings. It was turned into a limited company in November 1933, and in this form obtained all the private hire work for Red & White in London. Also arranged by the General Travel Agency was the fixing of agencies in Paris to which Mr Nowell travelled periodically. Red & White even

began to operate on the Continent with a few tours. General Travel Agency was closed down with the taking over of Blue Belle as this gave Red & White a better base to work from.

As mentioned previously, the directors of Red & White were diversifying in the late 1930s into road haulage (as they still are, under the United Transport banner) starting with milk haulage in 1934 (now called Bulwark Transport). A start was made in January 1937 in purchasing the long distance road haulage concerns which became All British Carriers. Gerald Nowell became a director of another concern in the same sphere of business, London & Southern Counties Transport. This was renamed Pye & Counties Transport, still with Nowell as a director along with directors from Red & White, United Transport and some from the original company. If World War II and later nationalisation had not occurred the combination of all these road haulage interests would have made one of the largest groups in the country.

In September 1945 United Transport purchased Oxford-based South Midland Motor Services Ltd for £46,695 and it became a Red & White subsidiary. Red & White had started to acquire companies in this area commencing with Newbury & District in January 1944 and Venture in March

Two Red & White coaches are seen on location whilst on one of the film contracts negotiated by Gerald Nowell. Though barely legible, the wording on the luggage rack of the Albion reads 'Gaumont British Special'. The 6LW engined Albion with Northern Counties body [which still exists to this day in South Wales] shares the duty with an older AEC Regal acquired from London & South Wales Express.

1945. The company was hemmed in on all sides in South Wales and had to look elsewhere for expansion.

It is not known exactly when Gerald Nowell returned from the forces, but as the London companies were now under different control he was made General Manager of South Midland. Thus began the fourth stage in his career. In January 1946 he was also made a director of the company, but was no longer a director of Red & White, there having been a reorganisation of the directorships of the group companies. South Midland was one of the few independents to survive in the express coach business. It had been registered as the South Midland Touring Transport Co back in April 1922 as a coach and lorry operator. Coach tours only were operated until February 1928 when a service was started from Oxford to London, and the company was soon operating between Portsmouth, Oxford, Worcester and London. Agreements were made with Royal

A 26 SEATER OF OUTSTANDING ECONOMY

Three of the earliest Austin K3 coaches built shortly before the war were supplied – in August 1939 – to South Midland. They were hailed by their manufacturer as being 'the only coach with synchromesh gears', and South Midland's examples carried thoroughly modern Burlingham bodies.

The standard South Midland coach under Red & White management was the AEC Regal with Duple body, and a well-kept fleet of these fine vehicles was for some years a common sight on the London–Oxford road. Two early post-war specimens are seen here.

Hants & Sussex was operating a mixed bag of vehicles when Gerald Nowell joined it. A great deal of money had been spent in the purchase of many new Bedfords and Leylands but several older vehicles still survived in the fleet. This vintage Leyland TD1 emanated from Newport Corporation and was not finally broken up at Emsworth until 1953 although withdrawn from service some time earlier.

Blue and Red & White, working on the principle that it was better to work with the competition than to fight it. In 1936 a car hire service was started in Brighton called Britax, and by the 1930s the fleet consisted of Leyland Tigers, Cubs and Cheetahs, Gilford and – rather unusually – three of the earliest Austin K3 coaches delivered in 1939. Upon acquisition by Red & White the livery of the vehicles was changed to the group's standard colours and style, and Gerald Nowell immediately began to rebuild the business after the wartime recession.

Under Red & White auspices South Midland's vehicle policy was standardised with that of Venture and Newbury & District, featuring AEC Regals together with the odd Leyland PS1 with ex-North Western ECOC body and a couple of Bedford OBs, together with the inter-hiring of vehicles from other Red & White operators that was prevalent throughout the group. As well as re-starting the express routes, the private hire and excursion & tours business, which was Gerald Nowell's forte, went from strength to strength. Some tours stayed overnight at hotels owned by members of United Transport, proving the usefulness of diversification of business interests. In 1948 a through Worcester, Oxford and Brighton service was started jointly with Southdown, and this was so successful that a seasonal through service was commenced between Oxford and Margate jointly with East Kent.

All this success was to no avail, however, as the directors of Red & White United Transport had been negotiating with the British Transport Commission for the sale of the bus companies in the group, the directors being worried about the threatened compulsory purchase of their British road passenger assets. Gerald Nowell did not want to work for a nationalised concern and resigned in 1949 to start yet

another career with the expanding Hants & Sussex organisation as its General Manager.

Hants & Sussex was a peculiar conglomeration of small companies, all owned by Basil S Williams and trading under a distinctive red livery. Hants & Sussex Motor Services Ltd had itself been registered on 30th April 1937 and held licences in the Emsworth and Fareham areas. Under his own name, Mr Williams ran various acquired services based on Midhurst, Stedham and Graffham, whilst the Liss & District Motor Services Ltd was centred on Petersfield and F H Kilner (Transport) Ltd on Horsham. In addition there were three coach companies with no stage service interests, Sunbeam Coaches (Loxwood) Ltd, Southsea Royal Blue Parlour Coaches Ltd and Triumph Coaches Ltd, the last two being based at Portsmouth. The combined Hants & Sussex fleets comprised 130 vehicles at the time Gerald Nowell arrived (106 single deck, 24 double deck). Though to all outward appearances a major operator of some status,

Hants & Sussex was in fact a fragmented empire serving extreme points some 70 miles apart and with several isolated pockets of operation such as those at Fareham, Emsworth and Horsham.

Gerald Nowell had an important but difficult empire to run. Most operations were of a rural nature and, following the initial post-war boom, were beginning to lose trade. Nevertheless the business still had a buoyancy about it which resulted in the 1951 purchase of Empress Coaches (Stockbridge) Ltd (which saw Hants & Sussex buses running as far westwards as Winchester and Southampton) and Blakes (Continental) Tours Ltd, a Plymouth-based excursions and tours operator. Sadly, however, Gerald Nowell died at a comparatively early age. The Hants & Sussex organisation suffered an ignominious disintegration and final collapse in 1954. Perhaps Gerald Nowell might have prevented this collapse had he stayed alive. We shall never know.

Pride of the Hants & Sussex fleet were eleven modern Leyland Titans, three of which were sold to Gerald Nowell's former employers for their United Welsh subsidiary in 1950 as a means of raising capital. A Northern Coachbuilders-bodied low-height specimen is seen on the Fareham local service taken over from Glider in 1946.

Acknowledgement is made to 'London Buses - Volume 1' by Blacker, Lunn & Westgate, published by HJ Publications, for the story of Gerald Nowell's career up to 1927.

INDEX

Published by Frederick Warne (Publishers) Ltd, 1982
© 1982 Frederick Warne (Publishers) Ltd

ISBN 0 7232 2873 6

Printed and Bound in Great Britain
by Butler & Tanner Ltd, Frome and London

Albions galore. Double deck Albions, normally something of a rarity, always seemed particularly impressive when viewed in quantity as in this line up at the Parkhead depot of Glasgow Corporation. One is a pre-war machine rebodied by East Lancs but the remainder are post-war Venturers with bodies by a whole variety of manufacturers including Roberts, Croft, Brockhouse, Metro Cammell and Scottish Aviation. From their ranks emerges a modern, tin-front Leyland, one of a large number bought to replace trams and also many of the more interesting buses which once made up the Glasgow fleet.